YES.

simple response | radical results

Jared Ellis

yes.
simple response | radical results
by Jared Ellis

Printed in the United States of America.

Edited by Xulon Press

ISBN 9781498470858

Scripture quotations taken from the King James Version (KJV) – *public domain*

www.xulonpress.com

To my beautiful mother, who believed in me from the very beginning. You are my best friend, my inspiration, and my hero. I love you with all of my heart and I hope this makes you proud.

ENDORSEMENTS

BENI JOHNSON
BETHEL CHURCH, REDDING, CA

This book gives a very insightful teaching on leadership. Jared does an intriguing job defining the life of a leader using the well-known story of Joseph in the Bible. Jared describes the call, character and the process of a leader with the favor, successes, and failures. I found this book to be refreshing and heart felt.

JAYCEE JENNINGS
CHRIST FOR THE NATIONS, DALLAS, TX

"Yes." is truly a great book that is exemplified by the author and his passion for this generation. Read. Glean. Absorb. Repeat.

SCOTT BEARD
FOUNTAINGATE FELLOWSHIP, ABILENE, TX

This book is a great read for anyone who desires to fulfill his or her purpose in Christ. Jared gives thoughtful commentary to the life of Joseph by making it relevant and contemporary to believers who are passionate to know the Father at a deeper level. I predict this book will be the first of many greats by this amazing, young leader.

Table of Contents

Foreword

By Jaycee Jennings

Bible College. This is a place where dreams find direction. Christ for the Nations Bible Institute in Dallas, Texas, is a place that I have worked for years watching aspiring ministers come and learn the word of God and character development. Every year, I see hundreds of people with potential. They have the potential to do great things in the Kingdom of God. They have the potential to be world changers, history makers, revivalists, reformers and the next great leaders of their generation. They have the potential to be role models that show teenagers and children how to be disciples by how they live their lives to be more like Jesus. They have the potential to reach towns, cities, regions and countries. Each year, I have had the privilege of watching students graduate from this incredible institution with dreams, goals, vision and potential. However, all potential is like a well that needs to be drilled and tapped into. We all have to go through a lot of earth to tap into it and each layer has a different degree of hardness. However, all those who are willing to sacrifice the time to tap into their God-given potential will often find themselves standing at the door of destiny.

I remember Jared Ellis as a young bible college student full of potential, seeking the wisdom to unlock it and start on his journey to see dreams come true. He had a huge heart for people and a vision that was as loud as his New York accent. Jared wanted to see people come to know the love of Jesus Christ in their life and for them to unlock their destiny fulfilling their purpose on this Earth. After getting the opportunity to watch him on the pilgrimage that God has had him on, I truly believe that this book will bless every reader with life lessons from Joseph (and Jared).

My family has had the privilege of watching the author grow into an incredible man of God with character and passion through the years. I am confident that there is someone watching and praying for you to do something with the hidden potential that God has locked inside of your heart. You cannot choose your season of growth, but you can choose how you go through it and help others get through theirs along the way. May the Spirit of God unlock your hunger for greatness and give you the stamina needed to attain it so that you can live the life of a leader and truly unlock your destiny!

Preface

I hope that this book encourages you in several ways. First, I want you to know that you are not alone. I have sat with so many people, young and old, who have felt completely isolated in the midst of their process. So often, we can feel like we are the only ones going through what we are experiencing. One of the main purposes of this book is to do away with the myths and the misunderstandings of the call of God and to help you realize that there are others in this with you!

Second, I want to impart some wisdom to you to help you succeed in your call. I can promise you that this is not an easy road, and there will be many trials. However, God has given us a map, through the example of Joseph's life that can enable us to walk through the valleys of life with victory. I have certainly not arrived, but I know that God has given me nuggets of truth along the way that can help others avoid the mistakes I have made, as well as apply the truths that I have learned!

Third, and lastly, I hope to stir up a hunger in you to continue to dive deeper in your love for God and passion to serve Him. Being a Christian leader is an incredible honor and privilege. Sometimes when we serve the Lord, we feel like we are doing him a favor. This could not be further from the truth. God actually invites us to be partners with Him in running His family business.

It is kind of like a middle school 'group project.' We tend to be like the lazy kid that does nothing and gets the grade because there was one kid in the group who did all the work. We usually end up making more of a mess than actually helping God in His work, but God does not involve us because of what we can do *for* Him, He involves us because of what we do *to* Him. We drive him mad with love! He loves to involve us in his affairs because He so desires us to love what He loves.

No matter how high the mountain that stands in front of you seems to be, it is more than possible to overcome with the power of God that is inside you. I want you to remember something as you read the book, "God does not call the qualified, but qualifies the called."

I pray that this book helps you, encourages you, and pushes you to continue in your walk with the Lord in obedience and full assurance that He truly will complete the work that He started in you. You will make it!

God bless!

1

small-town significance

It was another Wednesday night in a little, West-Texas town called Abilene. Chances are, you haven't heard of it. If you're driving across Texas, you might pass by but you will most likely never visit. It is a simple town. Fortunately, God loves to do extraordinary things in ordinary places.

Youth Church, however, was anything but ordinary. A youth group that started with about 12 teenagers had exploded to over 200 students—ready and eager for what God might do in their lives each week.

This night was no different and you could almost feel the expectation in the air. As the pre-service countdown ticked away, students began to rush to the altar to secure their place for worship. The excitement was electric and as the lights moved back and forth over the crowd, I scanned the room and looked for familiar faces.

That is when I saw her.

I had heard about this girl from some of my students. (Although she has given me full permission to share her story with you, for the sake of her privacy, I will call her Jane.) Jane was in high school and was visiting our church for the first time. From what I had been told, Jane had a pretty rough past. I had not been filled in on all of the gory details, but I knew she had come from a broken family (like most of our students) and had a history of abuse. What I *had* been told was that she was a professed lesbian and that she had a rough history with church.

There she was, standing right in front of me. At the time, I was still leading worship at Youth Church and as the countdown neared the last ten seconds, I regained my composure and readied myself to lead over a hundred and fifty students into the Presence of God. "Five, four, three, two, one . . ."

Screams filled the room as we began to sing. It was just another ordinary Youth Church service but, for some reason, I could not keep my attention off of Jane. Instead of arms crossed and feet planted, Jane's arms were lifted and her feet moving. I had not seen a worshipper like this even among some of my most devoted students. She wept the entire service. It was truly a sight I will never forget.

Time passed and Jane kept coming to Youth Church. To be honest, this girl confounded me. On the one hand, I knew the lifestyle she was living and the past she had come from, yet I could not help but see Jesus all over her. Every week, Jane was up at the front pursuing Jesus with everything in her. I had no idea what to do with her, but she sure was messing with my theology!

None of this was a problem until Jane started having the desire to get more "involved" at the church. She told me (as well as others) that she had a passion to sing and lead worship. If I answered her request, this would mean Jane taking on a leadership role. I had no idea what to do.

The Lord began to speak to me about the call on Jane's life. He asked me to see her through His eyes and as I adjusted my perspective, I began to see the gold inside of this broken and battered young lady. Her "issues" became a lot less significant and her "purpose" began to surface. Instead of ignoring her requests, I sought the Lord for direction on how to go about integrating Jane into our core team. I had seen immense growth in her and serious changes were evident but, I also knew that there were tendencies to flop back and forth between lifestyles. I was scared that if I committed to providing her a place in leadership, she would break my trust and soil our reputation as a church.

Jane soon graduated from high school, which meant that she could no longer be involved with Youth Church unless she joined our young-adult leadership team. I brought her into my office and began to ask questions about her life, her past and her future. The passion that spilled out of this girl was astounding and left me incapable of ignoring the "Jesus" in her. However, I knew I had to address the elephant in the room. Instead of attacking the issue, I simply asked Jane how she was doing.

Jane was more eager to talk about her "stuff" than I was expecting. She explained to me how she had struggled with homosexuality in the past, but she knew that she was called by God and had a plan for her life that she desperately wanted to pursue. She told me that although the fight was real, she was committed to fight for Jesus. I just sat there, amazed at how God could speak to someone so gently and so clearly without my "help." Jane had encountered the love of Jesus that was calling her away from her past and into her purpose.

After that meeting, I felt the peace of God to invite her onto our leadership team as well as our Youth Church worship team. It was a risk, but the Lord had made something very clear to me:

Leaders are not perfect people; they are real people who have simply said, "YES" to God.

I also remembered that, years ago, God had taken a risk on me. I decided to return the favor.

As a result of joining our team and becoming a part of our family, Jane excelled in her walk with the Lord and her ability to lead. Her passion for Jesus was contagious and definitely something that demanded attention. In just a few short months, Jane was invited to accept a staff position at our church, working in the front office. She grew in favor with God and the people around her. She continued to pursue the Lord with everything she had. Almost a year later, Jane felt the call of God on her life to attend Bible School in Redding, California and was accepted by Bethel's School of Supernatural Ministry.

I will always remember Jane's last Youth Church service with us. I brought her up, along with three other students who were graduating high school and being sent off to Bible College. As I shared a brief, encouraging word for each student, I choked back tears when I came to Jane. I could not help but be overwhelmed by the testimony of God's goodness in this young girl. From a broken, confused, rejected teenager to a powerful, thriving woman of God, purpose had completely transformed Jane's life. It was more clear now than ever before: God can do a miracle in someone who is willing to simply say, "yes."

2

purpose in the process

A s you can see from the story in the previous chapter, God loves to write extraordinary stories from the most ordinary of circumstances. Over the course of ten years of ministry, I have witnessed God's miraculous power reach some of the most "unreachable" people, ones nobody would ever find purpose in. Something else that I have noticed is God's specialty in reaching and using young people.

One of my greatest passions is helping others, especially young leaders, become aware of their gifts, callings and ultimately, their purpose. I am a firm believer that everyone who is called by God has an incredible purpose waiting for them, if they would only seek it out! The beauty in discovering this is the journey itself. This is something I like to call, **the process.**

Throughout this book, we will explore together the story of Joseph found in the Biblical text of Genesis. Joseph was a young leader who was quite clearly called by God to do great things at a young age. Although Joseph's life was characterized by great authority, blessing and success—we must also look at the various difficulties and seasons of discouragement that led him to his promise. He, like the rest of us, had to endure the process to find his purpose.

Each season of our walk with God is another piece to the puzzle that leads us to the promises He has for us. Every move we make with God is another step towards discovering His plan and purpose for our lives. I believe He asks of us two things: first, that we are willing to say "yes" to Him when He calls us. Second, is that we are able to extend that "yes" in every situation that we face, whether it be favorable or frustrating.

When we respond with a willingness to do whatever He asks of us, God leads us by the hand and reveals His plans for us step by step. Saying "yes" to God is like saying "I do" at the altar. There is a specific and definite moment in time when we commit our lives to someone else, however, that commitment doesn't stay at the altar. Our "I do" must outlast our wedding day.

In the same way, our "yes" must persevere the process of God's plan. I can tell you that ever since I said, "yes" to the call of God on my life, He has asked me to do some ridiculous things. Although I will share more of my story with you in the next chapter, I can tell you that it is easy to start something. It is much more difficult to follow through and finish it.

Before we get into the meat of this book, we must first make the decision to respond to God's call. This is a dangerous and life-altering decision, so I ask that you take it as seriously as I do when I pose the question:

Will you say yes to God and will you keep saying yes for the rest of your life?

It's important to start our journey with this simple yet profound decision. One cannot go very far when following Jesus unless they have made up their mind, soul and spirit that no matter what the cost, their life will always respond to God with "yes." Difficult situations and hardships can never deter us from this resolve. It is the most powerful weapon we have in our arsenal and it will keep us steadfast in the seasons that try to shake us.

The story of Joseph will help us understand how we can effectively agree with God's purpose for our lives. The power in Joseph's story was not simply that he did amazing things for God. The power was in his "yes" at all times and in every season, even when it seemed like all was lost.

Understanding Your Yes

Another lesson we will learn from Joseph's story is how to understand the different seasons we will walk through as young leaders.

Along with our "Yes," we must also understand what we are saying yes to! God is calling us to a higher level of perspective. The 21st century culture we live in is bombarding this generation with distractions; constantly pulling our attention away from the things that really matter. To reach our potential and fulfill the plans God has for us, we must understand the seasons we are in so that we can effectively follow through with our decision to ultimately follow Christ.

In 1 Chronicles 12:32, we find the "sons of Issachar." These men where described as those who "had an understanding of the times to know what Israel should do." I believe that, to successfully walk in our purpose, we must have a Godly understanding of the times and seasons in which we live. This enables and empowers us to position ourselves to partner with what God wants to do in and through us in that moment.

Think of it like this: if a squirrel spends the summer seasons relaxing and enjoying the bounty of the land, he will have nothing to draw from in the wintertime, and will surely starve. If he waits until snow is on the ground to look for food, he will find none, and the cold will steal all of his strength. If he is not aware of other squirrels that might want to take from his stockpile, he might lose all he has! A wise squirrel knows what to do in each season. We are to have wisdom like this: we must know the seasons God is taking us through and position ourselves to live successfully in a Godly way.

Anyone who has been walking with the Lord for any number of years knows that following Jesus is not an easy thing. Never does the Bible promise the Christian life to be comfortable. We all must walk through trials that test our faith and strengthen our resolve to be true servants of Christ.

By unpacking Joseph's story, we will find keys that can help us in our own lives. The lessons we learn will help us identify the seasons we are promised to experience as young leaders and empower us to walk through them with victory.

Your Purpose Is in the Process

One of the most difficult aspects of being a young leader is our struggle with patience. If you're anything like me, you have a difficult time waiting on God. Another major preface I need to make before we move further in this book is helping you understand the "process."

It's a ritual of mine to make six eggs for breakfast every morning. Since I'm always trying to bulk up, I use my need for protein as an excuse to pig out on some scrambled or fried eggs. Recently, I learned a lesson through the process of cooking these eggs.

I would crack the eggs open, pour them into a bowl and whisk them until blended just right. After heating up the pan with some butter or coconut oil (if I was feeling healthy that morning), I would pour the eggs into the pan and start moving them around. The only problem was that it seemed like every time I made eggs, they tasted dried out, a bit burnt and half of it stuck to the pan.

One day I went over my friend's house and he decided to cook eggs for me. It seemed to take quite a bit longer than my process, but when the eggs were put on my plate, they were some of the best scrambled eggs I had ever tasted! They were perfectly moist, cheesy, and not a bit of it was burnt! I asked him how he managed to make the perfect eggs. He told me that eggs must be cooked slowly on low-medium heat. Patiently moving the eggs around at this temperature cooked them in such a way that kept the moisture in and kept the eggs off the pan.

You see, nothing that happens overnight is usually worth having. God knows that the call He has given you is something that must last your lifetime and because of this, He knows the process we need to walk through to live that call effectively. It's like the eggs—we are cooked perfectly by the fire of His presence and power when every part of us is slowly turned towards the heat. This takes time and many different seasons. I want to encourage you to embrace the process. Often, we want to get "there" right away, but as we read the story of Joseph, we will realize that certain lessons can only be learned through time.

Make a decision now to find purpose in your process.

You might not be where you want to be,
but you're not where you used to be!

One More Thing . . .

Before we go any further, I want to deal with one more thing. There might be some of you that are thinking to yourself, "I don't even know what my purpose in life is; I'm not sure I even have one!" Or maybe you're thinking, "I will never be more than I am right now; I feel the pull towards greatness but I don't have what it takes."

If that's you, I have good news for you. God has an opinion on the matter:

> *For I know the plans I have for you, declares the Lord, plans*
> *for welfare and not for evil, to give you a future and a hope.*
> *Jeremiah 29:11*

And:

> *Now to Him who is able to do far more abundantly than all that*
> *we ask or think, according to the power at work within us, to him*
> *be glory in the church and in Christ Jesus throughout all genera-*
> *tions, forever and ever. Amen.*
> *Ephesians 3:20–21*

Not only are the plans that God has for you so incredibly great, Ephesians 3:20 tells us that even what you ask for pales in comparison to what God wants to put into your hands.

I believe you were created for a purpose that is beyond what you can ever ask or think. I once received a prophetic word that said, "Write down your dreams and desires but do not expect to receive them. God will not give you what you ask for because He only gives gifts that are *beyond* what you could ask for. Expect greater things."

My heart for you in reading this book is that you would be awakened to the true call of God on your life. You do not need a prophetic word from a big-name prophet and you do not need a sign written in the skies. You have a promise from God right in His Word declaring that you were made for more. Every man or woman of

God—regardless of age, race, job, or position—is called to a life of purpose. Whether it is raising a Godly family and leaving a legacy; planting churches in nations all over the world; impacting culture through media and the arts; or building successful businesses that advance God's kingdom in the marketplace—you were made for greatness.

I believe, throughout this book, that you will discover practical and spiritual truths that will transform your life and encourage you in your own journey. But if you are doubting your significance, you *must* change the way you think about yourself.

If you go into this book with the mindset that you are a "nobody" with no call, no future and no capacity for more, you will fall into the devil's trap of disqualification and end up discrediting yourself. You will reject the revelation that is being presented to you. You may not feel like you are a leader *now,* but the truth is that anyone who belongs to God is called to lead. Leadership may look different for each of us, but it is leadership nonetheless. God has called us all to lead others to Himself and to do so effectively means viewing ourselves as leaders, as ones who are truly called by God. This is the true mark of purpose: those who have surrendered their lives fully to God in exchange for His extraordinary plans for them.

I believe the Lord gave me the chapters of this book as a road map, not merely a description of those who want to change the world, but a *strategy* for those who want to access God's master plan for their lives and see it become a reality. The life of a "called-one" is lived in the constant tension of failure and success, yet each moment brings us deeper and deeper into God's great design for us and our purpose. A surrendered life is no longer lived *for* itself, but it is also no longer lived *by* itself. God empowers the life given to Him to be a resource to all of those around it.

A life that says "yes" is a life that will change the world.

3

my story

L et's start from the beginning.
My parents were both heavily involved in church before I ever came into the picture. Mom (Barbara) had been raised in a Christian home and had decided to serve the Lord at an early age. Dad (Jeff) was raised in the Greek Orthodox Church, but was not personally introduced to Jesus until he met my mom. Technically, mom was not allowed to date anyone who was not a Christian, however, my grandmother made an exception for my dad, but with a catch: Jeff would have to agree to come over after each date and listen to my grandmother preach her way through the Bible and share the gospel of Jesus. Of course, with a beautiful young lady as his prize, dad had no option but to agree to these terms. He had no idea what he was getting himself into, but once he sat down to listen to his girlfriend's mom at the end of his date, he realized that something was missing from his life and it was not a girlfriend—it was a Savior. Through these late night talks, dad encountered the Way, the Truth, and the Life in the person of Jesus and accepted Him into his heart.

Of course, they ended up getting married. Before they had children, mom and dad served faithfully in their local church. They worked as youth leaders and ministered in any other areas that needed it (which is EVERY other area for a small, local church). A few years later, they decided to take a couple of months out of their lives to be sent as missionaries to Suriname, a remote country in South America, where they spread the gospel to the native people and lived among them in the power of the Holy Spirit.

In and around 1990, my uncle started Grace Gospel Church in Patchogue, New York. My parents came on to support him and the new church plant in whatever way they could. Being powerful leaders, they jumped in headfirst. Dad was one of the head elders of Grace Gospel, regularly teaching and preaching on Sunday mornings. He also wrote many articles, including a spiritual column in our weekly bulletin called 'Shepherd's Notes.' My mom was the worship leader and helped coordinate the musical side of things, all the while finding other ways to aid the church. This consisted of cleaning, organizing, administrating or singing "specials" on holiday services. Mom and dad were always right in the center of what was happening at Grace Gospel.

Though completely dedicated to the church, ministry was not all that mom and dad were a part of. Dad was a very successful physical therapist and started a few businesses where he treated patients and taught courses. Of course, mom was always right by his side supporting him in all of his business endeavors. Even when dad had to travel, mom was a strong pillar who maintained stability at home. They were a perfect pair.

I was born right around the time my uncle planted the church. I grew up with two siblings. Justin, my older brother, was my idol and my enemy all at the same time. We could go from putting on "Bible plays" and dressing up as David and Goliath to then having a full out brawl all in the span of ten minutes. Brianna, who we adopted from Korea when she was only a few months old, was four years younger than me and was "daddy's little girl." When Justin and I were out weeding the yard on hot, Saturday mornings, Brianna spent her time wading in the crisp, refreshing pool making sure that she reminded us that she was, in fact, a "princess" and "princesses" did not have to do yard work.

My First Encounter

My encounters with God began at a very young age. The first significant experience I had with the Lord took place when I was seven years old. I remember sitting in the church foyer waiting for my parents to finish up their worship practice for Sunday morning service. In fact, most of what I can remember from my early childhood consists of waiting for my parents to finish doing *whatever* they were doing for the church. Waiting has never been my strong suit, so I spent most of that time either getting into trouble or finding creative ways to deal with my ADHD . . . usually ending in trouble anyway!

However, this night was different. I sat quite patiently on the wooden staircase that led to our sound booth and spent a lot of time thinking. It only took one moment for those thoughts to lead to one of the most powerful encounters I have ever had. I suddenly began to cry. It seemed to rise up out of nowhere, but it flooded over me until I was weeping uncontrollably. I had no idea why I was so emotional until something inside of me spoke to my heart. It was a voice I had never really heard before but for some odd reason, I seemed to recognize it, like it had always been there. It almost felt like a veil was lifting from my eyes and I could now see a truth that had been hidden for years: I was a sinner and needed a savior.

Of course, I now know that it was the still, small voice of the Holy Spirit gently wooing me to a life-changing encounter with Jesus, but at the time, I was completely unaware of the importance of what was happening and the lasting impact it would have on the rest of my life!

After a few minutes of sobs and tears, I dramatically walked down the aisle to the front of the church and knelt down at the altar. My parents quickly joined me as they realized what was going on. We prayed together as I accepted Jesus into my heart. It was truly a moment that I will never forget.

The Year It All Changed

God's plan for my life began at a young age. We are so impressionable when we are young. God knows this, but so does the Devil. Just as God chose to grip my heart in my early years, the enemy had plans of his own to try to derail me. I am so grateful that God works all things together for our good (Rom. 8:28) and I am more convinced of this truth now than ever before, yet I can clearly see the ways the enemy tried to come in and destroy what God was building inside of me.

The News

I was ten years old when dad was diagnosed with cancer, leukemia, to be exact. He had just launched IMTS (Integrated Manual Therapy Solutions.) This was his own physical therapy company in which he could treat patients, teach courses and train other instructors who could travel and spread his curriculum throughout the nation. We purchased a building that would make this vision possible and were right in the middle of construction. During this time, it seemed as if we spent more hours at the building than we did our own home. We practically lived there. Building dad's business was a family affair and we each played our part: painting, spackling, laying new carpet, moving furniture, assembling furniture, dissembling furniture that had been incorrectly assembled . . . you get the picture.

It all started with a common cold. Dad began feeling sick, but he was not the kind of guy who would let a common cold stop him. He tried to overcome it, but the sickness eventually put him in the hospital. As the doctors gathered us all together, we received the news every family dreads: dad had cancer.

To be honest, I did not think much of it at the time. Growing up, I was told that God was a healer. He was completely good and could overcome any situation that seemed to be against Him. That was my story and I was sticking to it. Something in me just did not worry. I trusted God and left the rest up to Him.

May 18, 2001

May 18, 2001. To anyone else, it was just another Friday. To me, it was the day that changed everything.

I remember waking up and finding out that my grandmother was going to stay with us for the day. My mom had to go to the hospital to spend some time with dad and told Nanny (what we called my grandmother) that we could stay home from school.

I would have loved to go with mom to see dad since I had not seen him in about two weeks. Mom said that he was feeling pretty lousy and that we should wait a little bit longer before we went to visit him. Honestly, I was just excited to stay home from school! I remember lying on my living room floor with my brother and my sister watching cartoons, playing with matchbox cars and putting on Bible story plays without a care in the world.

Nanny was with us the whole day. She took care of us; made us grilled cheese sandwiches for lunch and even let us play outside. She eventually put us to bed and I determined that it had been a great day. Little did I know that I would wake up to the most devastating news that I would ever receive.

May 19, 2001

I awoke to the sound of crying. I got out of my bed and opened the door. The crying seemed to be coming from down the hallway. I saw my mother's door cracked open and it seemed like the crying was coming from her room so I began to walk in that direction. The hallway felt like it had been stretched out over miles and miles. With each step something in my spirit knew that I was about to walk in to an emotional warzone. A "grief grenade" was waiting for me, and every step further was just one step closer to the explosion. I opened the door and saw my mom and my brother sitting on the floor.

"Come in, Jared." She said, wiping the tears from her eyes.

I stood at the door; my feet could not move. I knew immediately that something was wrong and I replied, "What happened to dad?"

"Jared, do you know that I love you?" my mom answered.

"Yes," I said, as the knot in my throat began to well up.

"Do you know that God loves you?" she asked.

"Yes." The knot began to grow even larger. I could hardly breathe.

"Do you know that your dad loved you?"

That was it. With those eight words, my legs lost all of their strength and gave out from under me. I fell to the floor as I began to wail and scream and cry as my mind tried to grasp the reality that dad was never coming home. I had gone weeks without seeing him and would never see him again. My mind raced with hundreds of thoughts all at once: was this real? Is dad dead? Is everything I know about God a lie? How could He do this to us?

In that moment, everything I believed in seemed to come crumbling downward, bearing down on me with no way to escape. I had walked straight into that emotional war zone and stepped right on top of the grief grenade.

That night, after I had picked myself up off of the floor, I went into my room and decided that life was no longer worth living. After hours of trying, I realized that I did not have the guts to kill myself, although it was all that I wanted to do. Instead, I made an inner vow that I would hate God with all of my heart, all of my soul and all of my strength. I would never waste another second of my life serving a lie and trusting in Someone who had let me down so deeply.

Broken and Lost

Over the next six years, I pursued every possible escape from my inner turmoil. I was fatherless, angry, and completely disarrayed. I used and abused any substance I could get my hands on to try to ease the pain. I left the house looking for fights as an outlet for my rage. I got into sexual relationships to try to deal with my loneliness. I hated people, I hated God, and I hated myself.

During that time, I was diagnosed with clinical depression. I battled suicidal thoughts and cut myself regularly. I was deeply addicted to porn and spiraled into sexual perversion. I spent the majority of this time trying to balance a lie. To those in the church who I could use, I put on a fake, Christian mask. To everyone else, I made sure to let him or her know that I hated God and wanted nothing to do with Him.

I had no male role models to learn from. The pain of losing a father lasts forever, but for everyone else, life goes on. It felt like people had forgotten about what had happened to my family, and bitterness and hatred for those who said they would be there for us began to grow in my heart. I felt forgotten and abandoned, a pain that I would not deal with for years until God would finally sent someone to father me through it.

These six years were the most painful and empty years of my life. I had such anger in my heart that it consumed everything I did. Being incredibly creative, I tried to find music that would help me express my anger. This journey led me to the hardcore metal scene (screaming music), where I could feel accepted by the people and understood through the music. Having been a talented musician, a few friends and I decided to form a hardcore band and start expressing ourselves through this music.

We were the typical teenage band. We would practice in my basement and play shows wherever we could. My inner desire for significance began to grow and after playing a couple of shows on Long Island, we decided that we needed to go on a summer tour. I have no idea how we actually thought this would happen, being that we were completely horrible, but we were determined to make it to the "big times" and travel the nation playing our music.

We approached our drummer's mom about the idea, to which she replied that we could do the tour if we first attended a youth conference with her in New Haven, Connecticut. We figured that it would be easy. We would go to the conference, find some cute girls to hook up with, weather through the weekend, and then start planning our summer tour. So we set out to Connecticut to attend the conference.

The Call

The weekend in Connecticut was bizarre, to say the least. It was a "charismatic" conference and it was the first time I had ever seen anything like it.

Let me back up for a second. I was raised in a very conservative church that placed great emphasis on doctrinal teaching and theological correctness. I was taught that ANYTHING that was "Pentecostal" or "charismatic" was a direct result of poor teaching and false doctrine; basically, it was all emotional hype.

I want to say this: I am deeply grateful for the Biblical upbringing that I had. It grounded me and gave me a firm foundation for what I believe in, however, I never really had the opportunity to experience the "presence of God" in a tangible way, other than that time on the staircase, so, this was a completely new experience for me.

I had no idea what was going on, but I could tell that people were experiencing something at this conference that I had never experienced before. I could feel it in the room, something was totally different, but I was thrown off by all of the shaking, the falling and the weird language everyone seemed to know but me.

Stacey Campbell was one of the speakers at the conference. She was DEFINITELY different from the preachers I saw while growing up! When she would preach, she would get off the stage and approach someone in the audience that she had never met before and "prophesy" over them. She would tell them things about themselves that only they could know, but somehow, God had showed her too. To make it worse, her head would shake violently while she would do this. Again, this was completely foreign to me, but something about her was special. She spoke with such power and authority that it demanded my attention. I may have been a bit freaked out, but for the first time in church, I was not bored!

In the midst of the activity that was going on around me, all I could think of was, "this is nothing like my church back home." People seemed to be hungry for something that I could not identify. I was curious to find out what it was so I decided to stick it out and see what would happen next.

I stood in the back with my bandmates; black skinny jeans, colored hair, arms crossed. In my head, I thought to myself, "If this stuff is real, it is going to have to come and get ME, because there is no way I am participating in this madness."

Sunday Morning

Eventually, the conference began to wind down and the last service of the weekend was at its end. It was the Sunday morning service when the most unexpected thing happened. You know, the Sunday morning of the conference: it is the day when no one really expects anything to happen. It is the closing service . . . everyone is ready to go home. But that was not what God had planned for me. My moment with God was going to be unique.

The preacher called up all of the teenagers in the building and asked them to join together at the altar. He then called up the people who were over the age of thirty to surround them. He instructed the older generation to lay their hands on the younger generation and pray for them as a prophetic act of generational transference and unity.

Once again, a moment that I will never forget took place: a little old lady with white hair that was standing besides me placed her hand on my shoulder and prayed this simple prayer: "God, show him the plans you have for him."

Instantly, I heard the audible voice of God say to me, "quit your band, change your life, and get ready for full time ministry."

I cannot explain to you what really happened in that moment, but I know that someone took the "old Jared" and replaced it with a "new Jared." I did not fall out or flop like a fish. I did not go into an ecstatic trance. I did not even speak in tongues. But, something had changed on the inside and I was definitely not the same person that walked into that conference three days ago.

I left the sanctuary and approached my mom to tell her what had happened. Of course, she began to cry. She had been praying for me ever since I was a baby. Even when I turned away after having lost my dad, she knew the call on my life was sure. Now, I was finally realizing it.

The Aftermath

Ironically, even when I was stuck in my sin, God spoke to me. The week before I left for the conference, I had heard the voice of the Lord speak to me and tell me to go to a church down the road from my house with my guitar. I showed up with my band mates to this little church and walked up to the youth pastor on the night of youth group. I looked around and saw nothing but baggy jeans, metallic chains, and graffiti on the walls. My band stuck out like a sore thumb, but something in me told me to go to this church, so I was going through with it. I asked the youth pastor if they needed a worship leader. To my surprise, he replied, "we've actually been praying for one to show up."

That same week before the conference, I led worship at this youth group. I had no idea why I had been led to this church, but I figured it would be a good way to show off my skills and impress some girls, so I put on a good show. I even bought cigarettes from one of the students after the service. Typical Jared Ellis.

However, *after* the conference, I came back to Long Island with a fresh fire in my heart. I could not wait to show everyone how God had touched my life and changed me forever. Finally, Friday night was here and it was time for church.

That night, the youth facility was being used for a church event, so we were forced to have service in the main sanctuary. I could not play my guitar, so I got on the keyboard and began to lead from there. As soon as I started singing, something came out of me that I had never heard before . . . my worship began to flow into spontaneous songs and passionate choruses. I began to cry out for the presence of God to fill the room through prophetic songs. Something was stirring up on the inside of me and it was spilling out into our youth service.

That night, service ended at about two in the morning. This became a normal occurrence for us, and happened almost every Friday night for months. Our youth group was experiencing what I believe was revival, and our Friday night services became a place that not only teenagers would come and experience God, but also adults would make their way in to see and be a part of what God was doing.

Those nights were unforgettable. I remember students throwing drugs onto the altar in repentance, crying out for God to save them from their sinful ways. I remember spending hours in prayer and intercession over our country as we held the American flag over the stage. Week after week, we would gather to cry out for more of God in worship and prayer. It was truly remarkable.

As I look back on that year, I see now that God was doing something miraculous and I realize that what I had experienced in Connecticut was not an ordinary encounter. I had been called and commissioned to do the work of the Lord and wherever I would go, His mighty power would go with me.

Long Island Fire

While growing up, I attended a Christian High School. We would have chapel every week in the sanctuary. From 10th grade to 12th grade, I led worship for these chapel services. Every Thursday morning, we would gather for a couple of songs and a message from a speaker. It was like clockwork; every worship service was the same. We would sing three songs, pray, and be done.

However, after my encounter, my heart was burning to see a move of God sweep across my school. I began to lead out in prophetic songs, hoping that the students would catch on and experience the same outpouring that we were experiencing back at my church. Instead, they would stand and stare at me as if I had three heads. Out of my immature zeal for God, I would publicly rebuke my fellow students in the middle of songs for not worshipping. I would preach the fire of God and the need to move away from complacency. I would beg my friends to give themselves fully to Jesus. I was young and childish and probably handled those situations without tact, but I was passionately on fire for God and was driven by a desire for more of Him and a vision to see revival take over my school.

This passion burned so deeply that during school hours, I would end up reading my Bible instead of paying attention in class. I was so hungry for more understanding and revelation that nothing could get in the way of my pursuit. I would go to school and read my Bible, and then would come home and spend hours in prayer and studying God's word. During this time, I lost a lot of friends because of their disdain for my new lifestyle. A lot of my peers could not even believe that the "Jared" they had previously known was actually a new creation and was genuinely serious about following Jesus.

Regardless of my peers' perceptions, I continued to pursue God with everything in me. I traveled around Long Island from the ages of sixteen to eighteen, preaching the message of revival and leading worship for different churches and church events. I ended up returning to my uncle's church my senior year of high school and was given the role as the college minister along with two other friends. It still boggles my mind to think that I was a college pastor at seventeen years old, but a similar trend of promotion and favor beyond my years would follow in years to come.

We ended up starting a service for college students and young adults where we would worship and preach on a rotational basis. We saw great and powerful things happen, even though it was a small church and a small group.

God had changed my life and I was walking out the calling that He had for me, however, I still struggled with some personal battles. I had been introduced to porn when I was about seven years old when a friend of mine invited me over to see a video he had downloaded on his computer. It was a porn flick, and though shocking at my age, it planted a seed of sexual immorality in my heart that would continue for years to come.

From then on, I lived with a serious addiction to pornography. I knew that I was called to ministry full-time, but I constantly felt disqualified by my struggle. I eventually heard the Lord call me to attend Christ For The Nations Institute (CFNI) in Dallas, Texas, where a good friend of mine, Ben Schneider, had started attending a year before I had graduated high school. During my senior year, Ben came back to Long Island on a break to speak at one of our school chapels. He preached one of the most powerful and anointed messages about the love of Jesus I had ever heard. He spoke about freedom from bondage and true liberty in a life fully devoted to God. I remember experiencing the presence of God in such a powerful way that I knew I had to follow in Ben's footsteps and attend CFNI. I needed the freedom that Ben spoke of and something in me knew that by going to Dallas, I would experience that freedom.

Christ for The Nations

Soon after, I graduated high school and made plans to attend Christ for The Nations Institute. After witnessing a leader's fall in ministry due to moral failure, I knew that my call to CFNI was sure. I departed for Dallas in August 2008 and started my first year in ministry school. God quickly paired me with an incredible mentor who walked me through my struggle with pornography as well as my deep-rooted issues of unforgiveness towards past church leaders who had wounded me greatly. TJ and I would go on walks for hours as he listened to me work through my fears and failures. He showed me how to let go of my bitterness towards God and towards those who had let me down over the years. I began to release the pain and receive the love that only the True Father can give. It was supernatural, but the moment I stepped onto that campus was the moment

God set me free from so many of my addictions, not just to pornography, but even my emotional addictions to hatred and anger. God brought me to another level of surrender and consecration as I received healing and restoration.

While at CFNI, I grew at an accelerated rate and the same favor and anointing that was upon my life on Long Island seemed to increase as I continued to walk the path that God had set before me. I made it a discipline to get up every morning at 5:30 and spend two hours in the House of Prayer on campus. I truly believe that it is because of these times that God poured out favor and blessing upon my life.

Throughout my first year, I led worship and intercession sets at the Gordon Lindsay House of Prayer. I was quickly promoted in the areas of worship and leadership. At the end of my first year, I felt a call to serve Youth for The Nations, a camp for teenagers that was held by Christ For The Nations for 6 weeks during the summer break. At the time, it seemed like the last thing I would want to do, but I knew from experience that obedience to God brought favor and growth, so I spent my summer serving YFN. Throughout that summer, I had a double hernia and was encouraged to quit the summer internship, but I knew that God had something in store for me, so I weathered through it and completed my summer term.

God's favor kept increasing as I was given more and more responsibility. After interning my first year with YFN and finishing out the summer, I returned to CFNI in the fall and was promoted to YFN leadership and staff. I became the YFN Worship Director, one of the five main worship directors on campus. During my third year, I was promoted to the Conference / Assistant Director position of YFN. I was responsible for managing all of our traveling conferences as well as serving as the overseer of the YFN interns and leaders during the summer camp. YFN was an incredibly intense growth period as I learned how to lead effectively, communicate powerfully and activate spiritual gifts. During that time, I witnessed more supernatural occurrences than ever before. Healings, salvations, baptisms in the Holy Spirit and deliverances were an everyday occurrence. I was even put in charge of the deliverance ministry and had the responsibility of casting out devils (which was definitely a stretching experience, to say the least). In that time, I was honored to serve under Pastor Jaycee Jennings and glean from his wisdom and training.

At the age of twenty, I was offered the full-time position as the YFN Assistant Director. I had just recorded one of my original songs on the CFNI 37th worship album and everything seemed to be going my way. During CFNI's worship conference, I had the opportunity to connect with some of the worship leaders from Bethel Church in Redding, California. I began to feel a pull towards Redding to be a part of what God was doing there. The only problem was that I had just been offered the position I worked three years for and would have to leave my opportunities in Dallas to start from scratch in Redding.

It was a difficult choice to make: stay in Dallas and start my ministry career with YFN or move to Redding to pursue the "more of God." I had heard about what God was doing at Bethel and had a strong desire to grow in the supernatural, however, I would have to give up my dream job to start over and attend the first year school of ministry at Bethel. I knew that if I stayed in Dallas I could promote my ministry to one day be at the place I would need it to be to have great influence, but something in me desired to have a supernatural future. I wanted to be able to say, "There is no way I would be here without a divine miracle."

So I chose to let it all go and relocate to Redding. God always honors our decision to humble ourselves and let Him be the one to exalt us. I spent an incredible year in California. I experienced deliverance from spiritual pride, religion, and performance. I was forced to deal with my "orphan spirit" and had to learn to be okay without any type of ministry attached to my name. However, God was faithful to me, and continued to promote me in the midst of my mess.

I was asked to lead worship at Bethel's School of Supernatural Ministry and saw God open incredible doors for me while I was there. I made amazing connections and gleaned from some remarkable leaders. I was even able to travel to New Zealand and Tahiti to do missions work overseas. I watched as God moved powerfully in this season and proved His ability even when I felt like I had none. I had gone to Bethel to experience "the more" and was able to witness it with my own eyes.

I had the honor of preaching at a church in Auckland, New Zealand and during my message, a woman cried out, "Can God heal me from my cancer." I answered with a "yes" and watched as our Bethel team ministered to her. The miraculous power I had been searching for was right in front of me as we watched a woman's cancerous tumor disappear on her body. There were many other signs, wonders and displays of power on that trip, but I knew that God was calling me to move on.

As my year at Bethel began to wind down, I decided to start growing in my calling and take a pastoral role. With opportunities for me to continue in promotion at Bethel Church, I decided once again to lose it all to follow the call of God.

At the age of twenty-one, I moved to Abilene, Texas where I became the Student Pastor at Fountaingate Fellowship. When I arrived at the church, the youth ministry consisted of about 20 students who had no real passion for God. That was a problem for someone like me who had big dreams to see revival take over a city, so I got to work and sought the Lord for His plan and purpose for this ministry.

As some serious changes began to take place, the students who were not serious about God began to leave. I started to disciple the students that stuck around and taught them how to grow in their passion for Jesus and move in the power of the Holy Spirit. Youth Church was born, and in six months, the youth ministry exploded. The growth was immense. We never played any games and we never had giveaways. We simply pursued the presence of God in worship, and as we did God grew it exponentially. I am motivated by a belief that young people truly want a move of God more than they want a fun youth ministry. This core value was undeniably proven during my time pastoring at Youth Church.

What happened in Abilene was nothing less than revival. Students every week would flood the building to go after God and see Him move in unprecedented ways. Not only would they come to church, but they were bringing church with them to their high schools. Every week seemed like we had a new testimony of someone being radically healed and others coming to salvation for the first time. It was truly remarkable.

After three years of leading Youth Church and growing it to over 250 students, I felt God calling me to take six months and receive more training at another church. With the blessing of my senior pastor and a God-given replacement, I left Abilene to join the staff at Elevation Church in Charlotte, NC. I spent six months growing and learning, and although offered and opportunity to come on staff full-time, I felt the call of God lead me to move back to Dallas and pursue traveling ministry.

The Call

I am awestruck by the power of the call of God and His promise to my life. I have traveled all over the world doing things that I would never have imagined possible. I am truly blessed to be able to say, that at my age, that I have been a part of so much of what God is doing in the earth today. Many are astounded at my age when I tell them all the things that God has done in and through me, but I am not surprised. God uses anyone who is simply willing to be made available for His purposes and say "yes."

The truth is that the call of God will take you further than you could ever imagine. From the broken teenager to the leader that I am now, God has proven the power of His call through my life. There were many seasons of trials that I had to walk through to get where I am, but I would never trade those experiences for anything because I see plainly the power of the call of God and how worthwhile it is. It was not an easy journey and the journey still presents difficulties today, but I believe that God had me walk through those times so that I can share with you the lessons he taught me.

If God could use a mess like me, He can most certainly use you.

4

the call

Although I minister to all types of people, I specialize in working with young leaders because I believe there is something special about that age group that God loves and desires to use. All throughout scripture, God has called some of the most ordinary people to some of the most extraordinary things at young ages. Almost all of the disciples were believed to have been teenagers. Mary was believed to have been only a young girl when she was visited by the angel and informed that she would carry the very Son of God. David was just a young shepherd boy when he was anointed to be the future king over all of Israel.

God is in the business of calling young people to do great things. It was this way in the life of Joseph.

> *And this is the history of Jacob: Joseph being seventeen years old was feeding the flock with his brothers.*
> *Genesis 37:2*

Joseph was just seventeen when this biblical account begins. The text actually denotes that his call was being formed even earlier than the age of seventeen.

> *Now Israel loved Joseph more than all his children,*
> *because he was the son of his old age.*
> *Also he made him a tunic of many colors.*
> *Genesis 37:3*

So the question is, do you have to be young to do great things in the kingdom? Of course not! God uses individuals of every age and type to do the work of His kingdom, *but I believe that often times we see God using young people to remind us He loves using those whom the world would not expect.* It is important to remember that what the world views as "qualified" means nothing to God!

Joseph was called at a young age. This calling set him apart from the rest of his family. Being the son of his father's old age made him very special. You could almost call him a walking miracle. This gave him a special connection to his father, a special bond. However, even though Joseph's father understood and validated the unique calling on his life, not everyone understood or celebrated it with him. In just the next verse, the Genesis account describes how Joseph's brothers' viewed him and his "calling."

> *But when his brothers saw that their father loved him more*
> *than all his brothers, they hated him and*
> *could not speak peaceably to him.*
> *Genesis 37:4*

Joseph's calling did not make everyone happy. It stirred up anger and jealousy in his brothers and caused them to hate him.

We will talk more about this issue in the next chapter but for right now, it is very important for you to understand this truth about the call of God: *It is all the validation that you need.* The call is a very special and honored thing to bear; yet it is also a very weighty thing. On one hand, it brings favor and blessing. Authority flows from someone who is deeply called by God. However, on the other hand, the call brings envy, covetousness, and often times, much misunderstanding.

You may not have the approval of others. You may feel like you are completely unqualified to do what God has put in your heart. It may seem utterly impossible for you to go where God has called you to go. If that is the case, you are in luck. God calls the most unqualified individuals to work through to prove His power and glory!

So how do you know that you are called?

What is "The Call?"

The call of God is something that cannot be unnoticed or hidden. God will mark you. Just as Joseph's father did for Him, your Heavenly Father will dress you in a "robe of many colors." This "spiritual" robe is a powerful gift that cannot be taken back. It has been tailor made for you, specific to your very measurements and stature.

Your CALLING is found in your CONNECTION to God, your Father!

The call means many things. The first meaning of the call is found in our identity. Knowing that we belong to God empowers us to do anything that is set before us. Having a close, intimate relationship with the Creator of all things reminds us that nothing is impossible and we were made for more.

The second meaning of the call is our God-given purpose. From our identity stems our destiny. We draw from who we are to accomplish what we are called to do. That calling is specific to YOU and no one can take it from you!

The robe that Joseph wore would not fit anyone else's body; it was specifically made for Joseph. Obviously, the robe represents something more than just a piece of clothing. The robe that God gives you is your calling! Your call is not something you earned or asked for; God gave it to you because you are His! It was not meant for anyone else to try on or to take from you, it was designed for you alone! You need not borrow anyone else's robe. You have one that is made just for you! You may feel unworthy or unqualified, but you have a Father who does not seem to think so!

God does not choose people based on earthly gifting, talent, or qualifications. I have often heard it said, "God does not call the qualified; He qualifies the called." Check out what Paul tells us in his letter to the Corinthians:

"Instead, God chose things the world considers foolish in order to shame those who think they are wise. And he chose things that are powerless to shame those who are powerful."
1 Corinthians 1:27

Maybe you are just like Joseph, an ordinary kid, the baby of the family. He seemed to be nothing special. He was born into the same family as his brothers and shared the same life that they had. In the natural, Joseph did not have anything more than his brothers had, but in the Spirit, Joseph had something unique to him: a call from God that set him apart and a "YES" in his heart.

All you need is a call from God and a willingness to say "yes" that call to truly accomplish great things. It is not an easy road. Joseph had no idea what was ahead of him! But, God had equipped him with everything he needed because ultimately, it was GOD'S call, not his. There is peace and power in the trust we have in God's promise to complete the work He started in us.

Here is some really good news:

> *The one who calls you is faithful, and He will do it.*
> *1 Thessalonians 5:24*

Call-Killers

So, what can keep us from really living in the fullness of our calling?

Well, for one, we can resist the gift of God. I am sure there were times when Joseph felt like the last thing he wanted to do was to wear that robe his dad had made for him. All he would receive in return was jeering and mocking from his brothers. It would be easier to just hide it away and live a normal life.

This never really works, because God is far more persistent than we are and He desires for us to receive His good and perfect gifts. However, He allows us to choose to receive His call. We can hide it or reject it, but it is still always there.

So why would we ever reject the call of God?

Well, sometimes the call of God means standing out. That colorful robe definitely did not blend in with rest of the family's clothes. To wear it meant to stand out and to make a statement, and sometimes we do not want to make any statements. Sometimes we just want to stay in the shadows and "fit in." Life is much easier when you can blend in and be normal.

***As a young leader, you are not called to FIT IN;
you are called to STAND OUT.***

We could also use the robe for purposes that it was never meant for. Instead of wearing it, we could hang it up as a trophy. I mean, it is beautiful, right? You might as well show it off.

The truth is that the robe was never designed to be displayed as a trophy where moths can come and destroy it. You were meant to *wear* the robe. It is meant to go with you wherever you go, not just to the places you would like to show it off. It must become a part of your lifestyle, not just a piece of laundry.

The second way we can resist the gift of God is by squandering it. Joseph's robe was quite expensive and communicated great wealth. Instead of wearing it, he could have sold it for a small fortune and purchased what he really wanted.

Often times we want to squander what God has given us to pursue our own desires. Until we have fully accepted and received God's gift, we cannot fully walk out God's plans for us. This means embracing His gift wholeheartedly, not desiring anything but His purposes.

Lastly, and most importantly, we can forget whom we belong to. Knowing that our Father is the King of kings reminds us that no matter what season of life we are in, we are connected to the most powerful and loving Father who ever existed. This is where the call originates from.

Identity always precedes purpose.

As young leaders, we must make exploring our identity the utmost priority. Why? Because despite age, God has called you to set an example for others.

> *Don't let anyone look down on you because you are young,*
> *but set an example for the believers in speech, in conduct,*
> *in love, in faith and in purity.*
> *1 Timothy 4:12*

Yes! You might have less life experience than others and yes, you might not have as much education. What truly matters is the fact that you have the Holy Spirit of God living on the inside of you who longs to reveal to you your true identity in Christ. Not only is God waiting for you to realize your true potential, the Bible tells us that all creation is longing for you to awaken to the purpose God has for you.

For the creation waits in eager expectation
for the children of God to be revealed.
Romans 8:19

Understanding your calling is the single most important key you can obtain to move forward in your purpose. It is the framework that holds the grand design of your future in place.

On one side of the coin, we see the promises of God and we live in eager expectation of what He has called us to do. On the other side of the same coin, we see all the reasons it seems impossible for that call to come to fruition. Do not disqualify yourself because the call seems too big. There is no call bigger than the God who gave it to you!

Activation:

What is the robe (call) that God has asked you to wear? Have you been hesitant to put it on because you feel unworthy? Have you kept it in the closet because you are afraid of what others may think of you? Stop disqualifying yourself and let the Father dress you in the robe of His calling and grace. Fully embrace His plan for you!

Prayer:

God, reveal to me your greatness and your faithfulness. I recognize that the call on my life seems impossible with man, but with you, all things are possible. I put my trust in you for my future, my calling and my purpose. I fully embrace everything that you have for me!

5

walking in favor

The idea of favor has always intrigued me. Webster's Dictionary defines favor as the "preference for one person over another." I do not know if you are like me, but the very definition of the word seems "unfair."

As I look back on my life, I can most definitely see the favor of God in every situation. It was almost as if I received things that I did not deserve, for no reason whatsoever. I have been presented with many opportunities that far exceeded my "pay grade." God has never failed to open doors for me everywhere I go—and it has never been that way because I am worthy of it. So where does favor come from?

I began to ask God for revelation on the subject of favor. I believe that every Christian can walk in this type of favor and He started to show me that His favor is His way of marking His children and proving His glory through them.

We can see this in the life of Joseph. Joseph was known as his "father's favorite" from the beginning of his life. Genesis 37 starts the story by describing Joseph as the "son of his father's old age." This made Joseph very special to his father, and because of this unique relationship, Joseph's father (Jacob) loved him very much. The writer of the story even says that he "loved him more than all his other sons."

And there it is: that unfair, unsettling phrase. It almost seems offensive that a father would love one son more than the others, but if we really search the human condition, the idea is found to be quite common.

Before I describe favor's effect on our lives, I want to describe two types of favor we will experience as young leaders living for God.

Donated Favor

The first type of favor is *donated*. Donated favor is a gift, given freely by the giver.

If you are a Christian, you have received "donated favor." This type of favor completely confounds the natural order of the means by which we do things. In our human world, we work to receive something, yet in the spiritual world, God gives us what we do not deserve. This is the very definition of grace: unmerited and undeserved favor.

The Greek word for grace is *charis*, which can also be translated as "gift." If you are a child of God, by (spiritual) birth you have received this undeserved favor. This ridiculous, unearned, and unmerited favor paves the way for us to see the goodness of God play itself out in our lives. Not only is this favor for our own good, but when God's children walk in it, He is glorified as a good Father.

A good, Biblical example of this favor is found in the story of the prodigal son (see Luke 15:11–32). The prodigal had done nothing but squander his father's inheritance. He was completely unworthy of any gift his father would bestow upon him, yet he received more in a moment than he could ever receive in a lifetime. Through the goodness of his dad, the prodigal was clothed in favor, undeserved and unearned. This favor exceeded any understanding or earthly wisdom because it completely opposed how "rewards" normally work. It was a raw display of kindness, forgiveness, and unconditional love. His father had chosen him, and there was literally nothing he could do about it.

David is also a good example of this favor. When Samuel (see 1 Samuel 16) journeys to the house of Jesse in search of God's anointed one to be king, none of Jesse's sons were chosen except for David. He had done nothing to merit the anointing from the prophet other than God's favor upon His life.

You also, have been given this favor and realizing it will empower you to do more than you could ever imagine.

I'll never forget the first time I flew first class. I fly quite a bit, since I travel often, but I had never flown first class until a few years ago. I was actually flying home for Christmas and my mom called me the day before to tell me that she had, as a Christmas present, purchased a first class flight for me from Dallas to NY. I was ecstatic, although I will be honest, I had no idea what the difference was other than the little curtain that separated the two sections.

The next day, I got to the airport and waited in the terminal, eager to experience first class. As they began to board, I realized that my section was able to board earlier than everyone else. That alone was enough for me—I was always worried that I wouldn't have enough room for my bag in the overhead bin so this was definitely a step up. As I entered the plane I looked and saw my seat—1A. I had never been that close to the pilot before! Not only was I the first seat on the plane, I had more leg room than I knew what to do with!

I sat down and checked out all the cool features in my seat. I had a special little table connected with a magazine drawer on the side. There was a TV in front of me and the seat reclined further back than seats in coach. If that wasn't enough, everyone entering the plane looked at me like I was either famous or really rich. Of course, I was neither . . . but they didn't know that.

Soon after I sat down, the stewardess came up to me and asked if I would like a hot towel. I was blown away. Of course I did! Then she asked me what I would like to drink. I ordered a coffee with cream and two sugars. This was the life!

After she came back with my drink, she asked me and my first-class neighbor if we wanted food. I said no because I didn't have the money to pay for the $20 meal I saw on the menu. The guy next to me ordered steak. I was a bit jealous, but decided not to get too upset because I was already experiencing so much joy from first class.

After my neighbor got his meal, I couldn't help but salivate when I saw that NY strip on his plate. He must have caught me staring at the food because he looked up and asked me, "Are you hungry?" Embarrassingly, I responded, "Yeah, but the food here is so expensive and I've already been blown away by the service. I'm OK."

He looked at me with a smile and said, "Buddy, you're in first class. Your food is free."

Many of us are living OK lives when we could be living extraordinary lives, we simply don't know what belongs to us. God's favor is like first class and, due to a lack of knowledge, we can settle for coach. The only way to live in God's abundant blessing is to become aware of the favor He has already bestowed upon us.

Developed Favor

The second type of favor is developed. Developed favor is built over time through relationship and closeness.

By answering the call and doing what God has asked them to do, there are those who have pressed in to the heart of God and have moved Him deeply. They have searched and sought after truths of the God and are constantly seeking His face, believing they will receive their reward (Heb. 11:6). Because of this, God pours out even more of His favor upon their lives and blesses them.

This is illustrated in a family setting. Though parents say that they love all of their children the same, you can always tell the ones they gravitate towards the most. Their *commitment* to and *love* for all of their children may be equal, but their *affection* for one will vary based upon the relationship and the connection they have with the child. Over the years, they may develop a relationship with one child who is more willing and open, thus resulting in a unique and deep affection for one another.

As a teenager, my mom and I had a tough time relating. I was angry at the world and did not like being vulnerable in front of anyone, especially my mom. Because we were so similar, my mom and I spent a lot of time fighting. We were two hardheaded Italians who had no problem raising our voices and battling it out. However, there was a turning point in our relationship when I had matured enough to really connect with my mom and we stopped fighting and started connecting. From then on, our relationship grew and developed to an incredible friendship.

My mom's love for me never changed, but her affection for me and her relationship with me developed as we grew closer together.

This is also illustrated in the life of Jesus. In Luke 2:52 it says that as a child, Jesus "grew in favor with God and with man." Even the Son of God, through consistent relationship with His Father, developed favor.

This perplexing notion that one could have more favor with God than another is quite insulting to the Western mind, but in all reality, it is a principle that the Bible teaches. Yes, when Jesus purchased our redemption on the cross, every spiritual blessing was made available to us (see Ephesians 1). We have all traded places with Jesus and received His reward, yet there are some people who have chosen to search out this reward and fully activate it in their lives more than others.

It is very important to realize that this favor is not EARNED. It is DEVELOPED. The two are quite different. "Earned" means that you worked for it and deserve it. "Developed" means that as you grew in relationship and intimacy with God, favor grows as a byproduct of that closeness. However, if we think that we can work for it, we can end up missing out on God's favor and end up with frustration.

We see this type of favor in the story of the prodigal son as well, but instead of the focus being on the prodigal, let's focus on the older brother. After spending some time out in the world and ultimately finding himself in a mud-pit with pigs, the prodigal realizes that it is time to come home. As soon as he arrives, his father runs out to meet him. Much to the older brother's dismay, the father wraps his arms around the boy, puts a robe on his back, a ring on his finger, and orders his servants to throw the biggest party of the year. Remember, this is a perfect example of the *donated favor* that we already talked about, however, the older brother illustrates *developed favor* perfectly.

He pulls the father aside and shares his frustrations with him. "I have worked for you my whole life and you have never thrown me a party like this! What gives?"

The father reminds him that the boy's inheritance was never something to be worked for; it simply came by association. As his sons, each brother had EVERY bit of the father's estate available to him. The older brother was just too busy working for it and not receiving it through relationship. If he had just *spent time* with his father, maybe he would have been able to activate his inheritance earlier!

If you have not recognized a supernatural favor in your life, it is because you have ignored your supernatural connection to God. Your Father owns the entire universe. Knowing Him and investing in your connection with Him is what activates an awareness of favor on your life.

Even favor that is developed is never worked for, it is simply realized through relationship. Our Heavenly Father has made every bit of His inheritance available to us . . . it is just those of us who truly get to know Him that get to partake in the riches of His glory!

Joseph's Favor

I am convinced that Joseph walked in both types of favor, however, I believe the text begins his story revealing more about his *donated favor* than what he would later *develop*. It is important to realize that Joseph's favor started from birth. We have no evidence that in the beginning of his life Joseph did anything to earn the favor his father bestowed upon him except for being his son. It tells us that because he was conceived and born while Jacob was an old man, he held a special place in his father's heart. Did he grow in that favor through relationship with his dad over time? I am sure of it. But it did not start there. It started because he was Jacob's son.

It is critically important to understand where your calling comes from and how you received it. It is from that place that you will find identity, and if it is not the truth, you will find yourself looking for identity in all the wrong places. Knowing that favor starts with *sonship* can empower you to not only walk in favor, but also to grow in favor. Remember, identity always preceded purpose.

Joseph was given great favor simply because he was his father's son. He was incredibly special to his dad, who spared no expense in showing it by clothing him in a coat of many colors (an expensive and expressive gift of high status and favor). Joseph never asked for this favor. He did not choose it. He did not work for it. His father made up his mind about Joseph the day he was born. This was his son in whom he was well pleased and he was going to lavish blessings on him no matter what.

There are two reasons why this revelation is so significant. First, it is astonishing to grasp the idea that simply because we are children of a Great Father, we are favored. That is incredibly powerful. Knowing that God has chosen us and made available to us His entire inheritance activates radical favor that surpasses our understanding. Growing in that favor is simply a byproduct of recognizing it and receiving it through intimacy with our Father.

Second, it is important to understand this because sometimes we can forget where our favor comes from. We can begin to take credit for something that we did not earn, work for or ever deserve. Everything we receive from God is a gift and a testament to *HIS* goodness and grace. Even the opportunity to grow in favor is a gift from God. Remembering this keeps us in a place of humility. It alleviates the pressure we feel to perform for God's favor! It is free!

So what do we do with the favor that God grants us?

The Favor Effect

Joseph never denied the gracious gifts his father gave him; he said "YES" to favor! I am sure he felt uncomfortable at times, but He fully received the favor that his father clothed him with. He did not hide the robe in his closet in fear of what others might say about him. He wore it proudly and showed off what his father had given him. He became a walking billboard, fully proclaiming who his dad was! A man or woman who is confident in their relationship with their heavenly Father is unapologetic for the favor that He bestows upon their life.

Knowing who your God is will result in knowing who you are.

Those who are confident in who they are and the favor they have received are aware that it was given to them freely. Even if the favor was developed over time, a confident son or daughter wears that favor proudly to show off their *FATHER'S* goodness, not simply their own. It is a public declaration to the world around them that they belong to a God who showers them with blessing even when they do not deserve it.

You may have found in your life that there is a supernatural favor which seems to follow you wherever you go that cannot be explained. Receive it! I recognized and identified a favor on my life even at a young age that I never asked for, but was obviously supernatural. I have seen the favor of God promote me beyond my years in every seasons of my life, even when it made no sense. I have had some incredible opportunities that I certainly did not deserve, it seemed as if I was wearing a supernatural coat of many colors that allowed me access to amazing opportunities all around me!

Whether these open doors came as gifts or came through developing my favor with God through relationship, they were all opportunities for me to display the very *GOODNESS* of God! Early on I realized that favor was a gift to display His power in and through me. Walking in that favor glorified my Father in Heaven more than I could ever imagine! He truly was displayed as the "God of the impossible!"

Yet, just like Joseph, there will be people who will make attempt to make you feel guilty for wearing your coat of many colors. There were plenty of times when I felt ashamed for receiving the favor that God had for me. I felt like I needed to hide it so that others would not get upset or jealous.

Do you remember in high school when you would get a good grade on a test that everyone else seemed to bomb? The moment you excitedly showed your grade to others, some kid made fun of you for being a nerd or studying too hard. It almost became "uncool" to get good grades because of the mocking you would receive if you did well.

This is human nature. Whenever someone succeeds at something, there are always people ready to bring them down. No one wants to fail alone, and the more people they can convince that failure is normal, the less alone they feel.

It is the same thing with the favor that is on your life. Those around you who do not walk in the same level of blessing will be quick to mock and ridicule you. They will try to do whatever they can do to get you to feel that your success is something to be ashamed of.

The Lord convicted me about this one morning. He spoke to me in my prayer time and said,

"Jared, it is MY favor. You are not responsible for apologizing or explaining why I am opening doors for you; all you need to do is walk through them and glorify me through your obedience. Your success proclaims My success."

Walking in favor is not arrogance as long as you recognize it as GOD'S favor. There is nothing wrong with realizing that God has marked you with something special, something extraordinary. By receiving this favor, you are proclaiming the goodness of your heavenly Father!

Young leader: He has anointed you for this specific call! Do not fall into a false humility that rejects and ignores the call of God on your life or His power and ability in you to carry it out. True humility realizes the call, celebrates the call and pursues it whole-heartedly! Ultimately, this brings honor and glory to Jesus because it draws others to Him! It is a testimony that reminds us that everything we have comes from God. We have nothing good in that of ourselves, but in Christ, we have every good thing!

<u>*Activation:*</u>

Are you walking in the fullness of the favor God has for you? Take some time to evaluate the favor you have already seen in your life. Thank Him for the doors He has opened and allowed you to walk through.

<u>*Prayer:*</u>

Thank you, God, for all that you have done for me in my journey thus far. You have truly shown your faithfulness and grace in my life when it seems like it was the last thing I deserved. Continue to lead me in the paths you have for me and help me lead with confidence and humility in the favor you have given me.

6

dreams of destiny

Dreamers have always intrigued society. Their creative minds and captivating personalities inspire and motivate us to dream along with them. They blur the lines of normalcy with visions of greater opportunities and possibilities. They are our artists, architects, developers, scientists and entertainers. In almost every area of life, they break the rules of regularity. They imagine a greater world and spend their days dreaming about how to change the status quo. Dreamers are anything but normal.

Steve Jobs was a great example of a dreamer. Never content with what the present had to offer, he always had his mind set on the future and what could be possible. Because his dreams eventually became reality, the world we know has been changed forever. Through inventions like the iPhone, iPod, iPad, and iMac, Jobs revolutionized the way we live and communicate every day. His dreams truly became a reality.

I have watched and read many documentaries and articles on the life of Steve Jobs, and they all describe him the same way: he had an eccentric personality and was extreme in his thinking. He always raised the bar and pushed the envelope of what was possible, and was often misunderstood. However, there was always a similar theme in his train of thought: do what has never been done before.

Some people have a hard time understanding dreamers like these. The truth is, we were not all created with the same type of mind. I am grateful for those who think structurally and chronologically; they like numbers and graphs and get excited about things like Microsoft

Excel. But, there are others who have more creative minds. They think in possibilities and like to color outside the lines. Both types of people are necessary to providing a successful and progressive culture, but many times, the creative mind finds it easer to grasp and develop dreams than the structured mind.

The good news is that God releases dreams to every type of mind there is. Whether you like numbers or you like colors, God plays no favorites and desires to give each of His children a dream if only they would ask Him.

However, there are some who have been given dreams and never asked for them. It was almost as if it dropped into their hearts one day and took residence without permission!

A Man of Many Dreams

Not only was Joseph given a dream without asking for one, his mind was arrested with the dreams he was given.

Have you ever been awakened from a dream that haunts you for the rest of the day? It is almost as if the dream was so real that you cannot seem to shake the emotions the dream invoked. It ends up dictating your mood and your attitude.

I have had dreams like this. I remember recently having a dream where a friend of mine offended me so greatly (in the dream) that I woke up in a cold sweat, furious with him. I called him up to tell him how angry I was and he laughed, but the funny thing was that I was actually still mad at him! I could not seem to shake the feelings even though the dream was not real.

This was the case with Joseph. He was a dreamer. God released two dreams (that we know of) in his heart that would shape his life and calling forever. His dreams were anything but normal; they were actually quite offensive. The two dreams that are described in the account of his life both have to do with his future and the future of his family. Arresting his soul and his spirit, these dreams made it impossible for Joseph to shake their grip on his heart and mind. He would *have* to discover what they meant. Let's read about what he saw:

Now Joseph had a dream, and he told it to his brothers; and they hated him even more. So he said to them, "Please hear this dream which I have dreamed: There we were, binding sheaves in the field. Then behold, my sheaf arose and also stood upright; and indeed your sheaves stood all around and bowed down to my sheaf."

And his brothers said to him, "Shall you indeed reign over us? Or shall you indeed have dominion over us?" So they hated him even more for his dreams and for his words.
Genesis 37:5–8

I Have a Dream

The first thing you need to know about your purpose is that you will be given a dream. God will place something in your heart that motivates, stirs and propels you to move forward and fight like never before to see that dream become a reality. Just like the dream I had about my friend, God's dream will arrest your heart and mind, taking residence in your soul and captivating everything about you. It becomes so real that it changes the way you see life itself.

I will never forget the dream that God gave me years ago in my little dorm room at Christ for The Nations Institute.

I was taking an afternoon nap and I began to slip into a light sleep. After having dozed off, I found myself in a restaurant with a couple of friends (in the dream, of course). I got up from the booth I was sitting at and walked over to the restrooms. Standing outside the men's room were three teenagers. Two were young men, one a jock and the other a punk rocker. The third individual was a girl. She was dressed provocatively and I remember thinking to myself, "Better avoid her."

As I walked over to the restroom door, the girl tripped me, and we both fell to the floor. I was so angry with her for tripping me that I did not even realize that at the moment she touched me, her appearance transformed and was instantaneously dressed in normal clothes. The expression on her face was no longer angry or seductive but it was excited and eager. She pulled me up to stand on my feet and said, "Come and see what I have been doing this summer."

My dream turned into a vision and I saw a newspaper clipping spin around until it landed on an article. As soon as I began to read it, I was transported into the picture and found myself on top of a large building. I looked out and saw a desolate land. There were many abandoned plains and the sky was dark. To my left I could see the Washington Monument and to my right I saw only a huge open field. I walked to the edge of the building that I was standing on and looked down; I was standing on top of the White House, however it was no longer white. It was brown, a wooden house soaked in water and falling apart. It was completely destroyed and abandoned.

As I turned around, I saw a couple of teenagers standing on top of the building about fifty feet away from me. One of them held a microphone and kept passing it to the others. Each would grab the microphone and say something that I could not hear or make out and then pass it on the next teenager in line. Once he had run out of teenagers to pass the microphone to, the man holding it looked at me and held it out in my direction. I hesitated. A teenager came out from nowhere and approached the microphone. Something in me knew that this was my only chance, and that I would never be given another one. I ran forward, grabbed the microphone, and immediately saw hundreds of thousands of teenagers standing in front of the White House, looking to me for direction.

Shocked, I stood there for about three seconds until a sound like thunder came from my stomach. It moved up my throat and came out of my mouth as a song:

"I will not sit by, I will not sit by, I will not sit by and watch my generation die."

I sang this song three times and watched as hundreds of thousands of young people erupted in prayer, intercession and worship. I knew that it was revival and I knew that it was going to come in the form of an army of young people. I awoke from the dream and realized that it was not an ordinary dream.

Years later, I can still remember it like it was yesterday. The song of revival still haunts me, I will not sit by and watch my generation die.

Personally, I was given a dream of a movement that would erupt from a generation that chose to consecrate their lives unto God. If

I had to simplify it, the dream God put in my heart is "revival." I live to see the church awakened to the real, tangible power of God. I dream of the day where signs, wonders and miracles are normal occurrences in the Western Church and thousands upon thousands come to know Jesus through a mighty move of God. Ultimately, I live to see a generation completely sold out to God.

When I shut my eyes, it is what I see! It is what I live for, why I do what I do. It is my dream, and ultimately, it is what drives me! God will give you dreams that are in fact His dreams, yet He involves you in them because He desires partnership above all else.

Young leaders know how to translate God's dreams to become their dreams.

He will move your heart so deeply that you feel *His* passion for that specific area of life, whatever it may be. It might involve something in ministry, business, entertainment, the arts, education, etc. It may be to see families restored or culture shifted, whatever it is, the dream motivates you. You become a partner with God in carrying whatever burden He lays upon your heart. First Corinthians 6:1 says that we are "God's partners, working together with Him." God invites us in as partners with His family business and offers us a share in His grand design to see change happen in the earth!

And when you get a dream like that, the last thing you want to do is to stay quiet about it!

"Bow to Me"

> *And his brothers said to him, "Shall you indeed reign over us? Or shall you indeed have dominion over us?" So they hated him even more for his dreams and for his words.*

When God awakens you to your purpose, he will invoke in you a dream that will shake you to your very core. However, it is also important that you know that not everyone else will understand or share this dream. Because of that, you must use spiritual wisdom and discernment to decide who is ready to partner with you in what God has placed in your heart.

Joseph reacted as any of us would. He shared his dreams with whoever would listen! This is common among dreamers. Even if their dreams seem to be offensive to others, keeping their dreams inside would be the worst punishment they could possible endure. Overflowing with passion and excitement, they spread the word to everyone around them, completely disregarding anyone else's opinion or emotions.

The interesting thing about Joseph's dreams is that they were legitimately from the Lord. By reading the rest of his story, we see that they were prophetic dreams; dreams that spoke of the future that was yet to come. However, in the moment, nobody really understood the full meaning of the dream because those events seemed so far away and so far fetched!

This is an area in which I believe Joseph made a huge mistake early on in his call. Joseph, much like any young dreamer, shared his dreams with his family. His passion spilled out uncontrollably as he described each picture that God gave him in great detail. Can you imagine this moment around the fire? Joseph begins to describe the dreams he received from God about his own family bowing down to him. How would you feel if you were on the other end of that story? Instead of being the one in power, you were prophesied to bow down your own little brother?

Remember when I told you about how my little sister, Brianna would tell me and my brother, "princesses did not have to do yard work?" This is probably how Joseph's brothers felt at the time. Joseph was standing before them, the baby of the family, informing them that one day they would all bow to him. This was not going to fly.

You see, the problem was not Joseph's dream; the problem was Joseph's timing and choice of audience. With a little more wisdom, I wonder if Joseph could have saved himself a lot of trouble.

While part of being a dreamer is certainly sharing your dreams with others, Joseph realized quickly that sharing his dreams with the *right people* at the *right time* would make all the difference.

Guarding Your Dream

Have you ever shared something that was so deep in your heart with someone you thought would understand, but instead, completely disregarded you? You expected them to celebrate with you or to share in your passion but instead they severely disappointed you. Maybe it was out of jealousy or maybe they did not understand what you were feeling, but they just did not seem to get it.

I'll never forget the day that I decided to move to Abilene and leave Redding, CA where I had been privileged with being a part of Bethel Church. As I shared in earlier chapters, Bethel Church is an incredible, international ministry that is known for its worship and movement in the supernatural. Although I had called this place home for a year, I knew that God had placed a dream in my heart to see an entire city come to know the gospel of Jesus Christ. It was burning with a desire to see young people rise up to a place of power and spiritual authority to bring hope to their communities.

I was eager and excited to move into what God had planned for me in my journey and wanted to share it with everyone I knew. I had received a dream from God about a city where young people would start a revival and this was the beginning of it! As I finalized the move back to Texas, I shared my heart and my plans with some friends in California who were not as "on board" as I was with my plans. Instead of encouraging and partnering with the progress of my call, they discouraged me and informed me that I was making a big mistake.

It crushed me. I was so expecting them to be as excited as I was, but instead they had the opposite reaction! It felt like everything that I was so confident about was now uncertain, and I began to question my choice to move on, even after God had made it so clear to me.

This is what happened with Joseph. The dreams God had given him were things that were spoken to encourage him about his future, yet not everyone around him was ready to hear it. Because of this, Joseph was deeply confused and offended by this so-called "God-given dream" of his. They quickly rejected and mocked him.

This is a deep pain for a dreamer. Dreamers desire to present their dreams in a way that will allow others to grasp them and partner with them, but when they are rejected or misunderstood, it is difficult to avoid feeling crushed and discouraged. Discouragement leads to confusion and insecurity.

> **Over time, we begin to question what God spoke to us in a moment.**

It is so important that you choose the people that you confide in wisely. WHO you share your dreams with will make all the difference. Sometimes the Lord gives us dreams for others that are harmless to share with them in the right timing, but not every dream the Lord gives you is for the people around you. It is common when we receive a radical revelation to want to share it with everyone and anyone that will listen to us. Our excitement to impart the news that we have received bubbles out of us but without wisdom, so we spew out secrets that the Lord intended for our hearts and our hearts only.

Let's look at what Jesus instructs us with:

> *Do not give what is holy to the dogs, nor cast your pearls before swine, lest they trample them under their feet and turn and tear you into pieces.*
> *Matthew 7:6*

Now this isn't a license to go around calling people who don't believe in you, dogs. But it is important to realize that not everyone will partner with your dreams nor will everyone celebrate them. Sometimes people are just not ready to hear what God has given you. Your dreams are like pearls that must be cared for and protected from swine that would trample them underneath their feet. We must ask the Lord for a spirit of wisdom and revelation when it comes to inviting people into our inner sanctum, the secret places of our hearts. As a leader, you may be a vision caster and you may feel like you cannot help but share with others the things you see when you shut your eyes, but knowing WHO to share with and WHEN to share it will protect you from those who will try to corrupt the dream inside your heart.

Activating Your Dreams

Joseph fully embraced his God-given dreams with an emphatic "YES." Here are a few ways you can say "YES" to the dreams God is giving you. These keys will help you understand, harness, and activate those dreams in a wise way:

WRITE DOWN YOUR DREAM

If you are anything like me, you forget things almost instantaneously. If I do not have a notepad or my iPhone next to me at all times, the thought that was in my head two seconds ago will be gone and lost forever. When you receive a dream, write it down and record every detail that you can remember. Often times God will give "progressive revelation" on things that initially make no sense, but after spending some time in prayer and thought, they are revealed to us. After you have written down the dream, spend some time praying into and pondering it.

PROTECT YOUR DREAM

It is important to take some time to really soak in the dream God gave you, especially if it is a significant dream like the one I mentioned I had at CFNI. I only shared that dream with one person but did not share it with anyone else for almost a year. Although the meaning of the dream was quite obvious, I wanted to make sure that I was a good steward of what God had given me. I protected it by hiding it in my heart and spent time praying through it. Do not share your dream right away.

One of the most powerful lessons I have ever learned was the message of the "secret place." The secret place is the place that only you and God share. It is your "secret history" with God and is special between you and your Creator. It is important to have things that only you and God know about. Just like intimacy in a marriage, certain things are for closed doors only. Make sure that you steward what God has given you well and protect it by guarding it against mockers and swindlers who would try to steal or corrupt your dream.

DISCOVER YOUR DREAM

Oftentimes we move quickly without consulting the Holy Spirit on what we are to do with our dreams. I have met with so many people who tell me that God has given them a dream, yet they have no plan of action or idea of how to make that dream a reality.

Spending time in prayer and asking God for patience will allow your dream to grow into a plan and eventually become a purpose. Asking the Holy Spirit to give you wisdom and understanding will empower you to make your dream a reality. Take enough time to allow the Lord to complete the picture. Sometimes God gives us a glimpse of the future that we think is supposed to occur in the moment, when actually He is speaking to us of things to come. Prayer and patience is the key to a successful dream.

SUBMIT YOUR DREAM

Although we have already mentioned that it is wise to know who you can share your dreams with, it is also wise to know how to submit the dream that is in your heart to those in leadership over you.

One of the most powerful things a young leader can do is find covering and stay submitted. You cannot truly walk in authority unless you, yourself are under authority. This translates into dreams: your dream will have no power unless you have submitted it to the covering and accountability of someone over you. Make sure you're not a lone-ranger or maverick. There's power in connection—take some time to get proper perspective by letting your leaders in on what God's saying to you.

ACT ON YOUR DREAM

A dreamer can become one of two people: either they stay a dreamer, a philosopher of sorts that only thinks of what *could* be done, or they can become a practitioner—someone who makes their dreams as reality.

There is an epidemic amongst young leaders in our generation and it's called "entitlement." The idea that everything is owed to you is absurd and anti-Kingdom values. Although we have been given an inheritance, God also knows that it is human nature to value what is worked for. Instead of waiting for someone to make your dream come true, start taking steps to see that dream come to pass. Only you can be the one to partner with God in your dream.

I first published this book at the age of twenty-three. People told me that it was impossible. I even had an editor tell me that I had no business in writing books. However, I had heard enough fifty- to sixty-year-olds who made statements like, "One day I will write a book." I knew God had called me to do it, so I did it. I self-published it first as *Unlocking Your Destiny* and put even more work into it so that you can be reading it today!

Take action on what God has entrusted you with. He is more than willing to be the wind beneath your wings—remember, it's His dream anyway!

ENTRUST YOUR DREAM

"God-dreams" are always impossible in human strength. If your dream scares you, then you can almost always assume that God has given it to you. The most important thing that you can do with your dream is trust God to make it happen. This obviously does not mean to passively wait around for it to drop into your lap, we are still partners and "co-workers" with God, but we must remember it was HIS dream before it became ours. Trusting God enables us to rest in His timing and power to make our dream come to fruition.

There is a fine line between working with God and working to promote yourself before it's time. I have always seen Isaiah 40:31 in two ways:

But they that wait upon the Lord shall renew their strength; they shall mount up with wings as eagles; they shall run, and not be weary; and they shall walk, and not faint.
Isaiah 40:31

Wait can mean two different things: it can mean to "remain inactive until something expected happens," or it can mean "serving" as in a waiter at a restaurant. I like to think that "waiting on God" is trusting Him completely, yet serving Him completely. Remember— He is faithful to complete the work that He started! Trust and obey!

Trust and obey
For there's no other way
To be happy in Jesus
Than to trust and obey.

John H. Sammis

Activation:

Has God given you a dream? How have you been a good steward of that dream? Who have you shared it with? Take some time to write out the dream God has put inside of you and ask God how you can steward it well. Use the four keys listed in this chapter to make sense of what God has shared with you and pray this prayer:

Prayer:

God, give me a spirit of wisdom and revelation. Show me the brothers and sisters around me who are safe to share my dreams with, but also show me how to be discerning with those who are not ready to partner with me in the dreams You have given me. Protect what You have put in my heart.

7

the killer of comparison

"How many likes did you get?"
"Are you following her?"
"My tweet got retweeted sixteen times!"

We live in, by far, the most digitally and technologically advanced age of all times. Not only has the smart phone revolutionized how we live our lives and do our jobs, it has made the world even smaller through instant connectivity.

Just think of how many people you see on Facebook that you never see in real life? Not only do you get to stay in touch with these people, you get to see all of the pictures of their newborn baby that you never asked to see! Social media is quite a concept.

I've never been one to hate on social media. I love the idea that we are able to instantly connect with people on the other side of the world through the touch of a screen. But one must come to the agreement that we live in the most critical and shallow culture we probably have ever seen. The idea that the picture we post is up for either a "like" or an ignore, (not to mention the hateful comments some leave) only solidifies a culture of comparison. We're constantly checking to see how many likes we got or how many people shared our post—all the while, lining it up to the guy or girl next door.

Let's face it: we love to compare.

Believe it or not, comparison isn't a new thing. In fact, it goes way back to the beginning of time. But for now, let's look at how comparison factored in to Joseph's story.

So far, we have covered three aspects of Joseph's story. We have talked about the call, the favor that comes with the call and the power of our God-given dreams. However, what happens when you end up sharing those dreams with the wrong people? What happens when your friends, family, or foes cannot handle the favor that is on your life and decide to turn against you? What do you do when there is an all-out war waged upon your purpose?

Let's continue with Joseph's story.

Now Joseph had a dream, and he told it to his brothers;
and they hated him even more. So he said to them,
"Please hear this dream which I have dreamed: There we were,
binding sheaves in the field. Then behold, my sheaf arose
and also stood upright; and indeed your sheaves
stood all around and bowed down to my sheaf."

And his brothers said to him, "Shall you indeed reign over us?
Or shall you indeed have dominion over us?" So they hated him
even more for his dreams and for his words.

Then he dreamed still another dream and told it to his brothers,
and said, "Look, I have dreamed another dream. And this time, the
sun, the moon, and the eleven stars bowed down to me."

So he told it to his father and his brothers; and his father
rebuked him and said to him, "What is this dream that you have
dreamed? Shall your mother and I and your brothers indeed come
to bow down to the earth before you?" And his brothers envied
him, but his father kept the matter in mind.
Genesis 37:5–11

After Joseph talks with his brothers, he realized that it was perhaps not the best idea to share *those* specific dreams with them. Not only did his brothers despise him, his own FATHER rebukes him in front of the rest of the family. Remember, this is the same father who empowered him with confidence and clothed him in a coat of many colors. Now, he was reprimanding Joseph for his outspoken disregard for his family's emotions. Everyone was frustrated with this dreamer and because of the message of his dreams, feelings of comparison grew in the hearts of his brothers.

My Issue with Comparison

I want to share with you my own story with the issue of comparison. While I was attending school at Christ for The Nations in Dallas, Texas, I had many moments just like Joseph and his brothers. A Bible college can be an incredible place of growth and development; however, it can also be a feeding ground for comparison and competition as young leaders struggle with their inner fight for success.

I have always fought with the demon of comparison. Growing up, I was the small, skinny musician who really did not fit anywhere. I never felt good enough or up to par with the expectations others had for me. To be quite honest, most of the expectations I lived under were self-inflicted, but I never realized it. I always looked at others as greater than me and envied their lives and talents. I tried to mimic them to find a sense of identity, but it never really worked.

It all seemed to change after I encountered Jesus. Following my experience in Connecticut, I began to find my identity in my pursuit of God and the call He had on my life. I was passionate and influential in my zeal for the Lord and people started to identify me as a "revivalist" and a "world-changer." I was very capable in my ministry and quickly realized that I could shape a life around it. A new found identity was formed in me and I centered myself on my ministry. I figured that I had finally dealt with my identity crisis and my issues with comparison were no longer a problem.

As I grew in favor and influence, I began to notice others who started comparing themselves to me! This was a first! Could *I* be the one that people wanted to be like? I could not have felt better about myself. I was finally free from comparison while everyone else battled with this inner struggle. Life was grand (so I thought).

However, I remember one instance in Bible school where my issues of comparison came back to haunt me. For years, I had often seen others as "jealous" or "envious" of my favor and calling; they were the ones dealing with comparison, until I met Jamal.

Jamal was incredible. Gifted, anointed, talented and most certainly, favored. Everyone loved him. I would have loved Jamal too, except there was a tiny little problem: he was being promoted and favored even faster than I was! He had no problem being outspoken about it, either. Everyone on campus knew who he was and seemed to fall at his feet for everything. Do not get me wrong; Jamal was a great guy who loved Jesus. I just did not get why everyone was paying so much attention to him and not to me.

I started to develop strong feelings of jealousy and bitterness in my heart towards him. I found myself comparing and competing with him internally. I would try to outdo everything I saw him do. I spent so much of my time comparing myself to him that I missed out on an incredible friendship that could have challenged me, humbled me, and propelled me into new places of growth and favor! Instead, I came up with excuses to ignore him and put him down. I tried to find fault in *him* when the real fault was in *me*.

I realized that the same issue of comparison that others struggled with towards me was the same issue of comparison that I was now struggling with towards him!

Now, years later, Jamal and I are incredibly close friends. After we left CFNI, we connected and got honest with each other about our issues with comparison. We asked for each other's forgiveness and buried the hatchet by deciding to partner with each other and grow in our friendship. We are able to laugh at the past. We celebrate each other's success as our own. We have worked past all of our immaturity and identity issues and joined as brothers to glorify God in our friendship, but our experience with the "Killer of Comparison" taught us both a very powerful lesson.

Don't get me wrong. Fighting the war against the Killer of Comparison isn't won in one battle. It is one you will have to fight for the rest of your life. Why? Comparison is one of the enemy's greatest tools and he uses it against those who desire to accomplish great things. If we remain unaware, it can obliterate us, take us out for good, and ruin relationships God has surrounded us with to keep us in good community.

Before we break down Joseph's brothers' issue with comparison, we must go back to the origin of this deadly disease.

The Origin of Comparison

It all started in the heavens with Lucifer. He was one of the chief angels, and instead of focusing on the assignment he was given, he decided to compare himself to God. He refused to be content with who God called him to be and instead, looked at his Creator and coveted the worship He was receiving. Lucifer determined in his heart that HE deserved that worship. Soon, that covetousness turned to bitterness. (This is how comparison always works; it starts and ends with "me" and when someone has something that I do not have or I feel like I deserve, I start making my case against that person.)

Well, it got Lucifer thrown out of heaven and separated from God for all eternity, but that did not teach him his lesson. Soon after, he turned his battle against God into an all out war. He entered the Garden of Eden and used the serpent to deceive Adam and Eve with the same lie of comparison that he told himself.

"God is keeping something from you. YOU deserve that fruit. He just does not want you to have what He has and overpower Him. See what He is keeping you from?"

Through the serpent, Lucifer planted the idea in their heads that they deserved more than what God had given them. The same "Killer" that got Lucifer kicked out of heaven became the same Killer that got Adam and Eve kicked out of Eden.

Comparison did not stop there. Continuing its destructive path, the same lie was then passed down from Adam and Eve to their own children. Because of comparison, Cain murdered Abel over a sacrifice that God preferred over his own. The issue of comparison has always been at the center of humanity's downfall and is without a doubt one of the enemy's greatest tools to destroy God's people and promises.

Comparison takes the focus off of God and puts it on self.

We were not made to be "self-centered" beings. We were created to behold the beauty and the splendor of God, to live lives of worship and adoration. When we start to allow comparison into our hearts, the focus shifts off Jesus and onto ourselves. This violates our very spiritual makeup and we begin to search for any way to find true identity. In ourselves, we have no good thing. This makes our pursuit for significance impossible apart from God and soon our eyes begin to drift off of ourselves and onto others. Just like Lucifer, we wage an all-out war to try and be the best, the smartest, and have the most significance . . . all because we have lost our focus on the true source of significance: Jesus Christ.

I am grateful for technological advances and social media that allow us to receive information at lightning speeds. It has enabled us to stay in touch with people all across the world; however social media is one of the enemy's greatest tools for comparison.

It hurts my heart and saddens me deeply to see how much of today's "evangelical superstars" use social platforms to promote themselves while Jesus seems to be somewhere in the shadows. We have learned to only post the best version of ourselves to deceive everyone into thinking that our lives are more exciting and exhilarating than they really. When all we see about people's lives is the highlight reel, comparison is almost inevitable. How are we supposed to live our lives focused on Jesus when we are looking at our phones every five minutes?

Matthew 6:5 says

"And when you pray, do not be like the hypocrites,
for they love to pray standing in the synagogues and on the street
corners to be seen by others. Truly I tell you, they
have received their reward in full.

Just change "synagogues" to "social networks" and "streets" to "tweets" and you have a modern day message!

Although he did not have Snapchat, Twitter, or Instagram available, Joseph shared his dreams with his family in an open forum and created an opportunity for comparison to grow in their hearts. In essence, Joseph was declaring himself "the leader." Not only were his brothers comparing themselves with *him,* I am SURE that he was also comparing himself to *them.* We often do this and hide it to avoid responsibility. We try to place the blame on everyone else because they are struggling with comparing themselves to us, yet in our own hearts, we are doing the very same thing, in just another form.

We say things like, "they just do not understand. I am on another level than they are. If they could just reach the level of favor that I have attained . . ."

This is a very dangerous road to embark on. As God's chosen, if you are not walking in humility, above all else, you can begin to slip into the deception that your call makes you better than everyone else. It distinguishes you, divides you and ultimately, it destroys you.

Jesus' Example

When you truly grab a hold of God's purpose for your life, you answer the call to leadership. In John 13, Jesus gives us an example of what a powerful, favored leader is supposed to look like. He dresses himself in servant's clothing, and bends down on his hands and knees to wash the feet of His disciples. The God of all creation, the greatest leader of all time is found washing dirty, stinky feet, even the feet of those will soon betray him! Yet Jesus' idea of leadership was far different from ours. His attitude is described here:

Let this mind be in you which was also in Christ Jesus, who, being in the form of God, did not consider it robbery to be equal with God, but made Himself of no reputation, taking the form of a bondservant, and coming in the likeness of men. And being found in appearance as a man, He humbled Himself and became obedient to the point of death, even the death of the cross.
Philippians 2:5–8

Jesus did not find it "robbery" to be equal with God. He did not put on false humility and reject His power and authority, but out of a humble heart, He served in meekness. He identified the call and the favor on His life and walked in it to the fullness, yet made Himself of "no reputation" so that He could serve others. I wonder what it would look like if leaders started making themselves of "no reputation" instead of trying to get every ministry success into "mass publication." Let me remind you that Jesus often told people to "keep quiet" after He had performed a miracle and they ended up writing a 'best seller' about Him.

You may not be able to control someone else's issue with comparison but as a leader, you can dismantle your own issues with comparison by serving those you are leading. This is the only way to overcome this deadly disease that the enemy uses to try to destroy your purpose.

> *The only way to kill comparison is to focus on*
> *others through the lens of a servant.*

Have you ever heard the expression, "kill them with kindness?" I remember when I was a kid I used to have a bus driver who was always miserable. (I will never understand people who enter the school system and do not enjoy kids, but this bus driver was definitely one of them.) He did not like kids and he definitely did not like me. I just could not understand it. I mean, who would not like a hyperactive six-year-old with a bowl-cut hairdo and a mouth that would never stay shut!

I was so upset one day after coming home off the bus that I cried to my mom. I asked her why my bus driver was so mean to me and what we could do about it. She told me to "kill him with kindness." It seemed gruesome at first but after she explained it to me, I was all for it! That night we made him a batch of chocolate chip brownies and brought them to him the next morning. For the first time, I saw my bus driver smile. It was working! We were killing him (with kindness, of course)!

After a month of polite gestures and small acts of kindness, my bus driver was the happiest bus driver in our town. Instead of feeding his bad attitude, we dismantled it through kindness!

This is how we are to handle the issue of comparison. We can either invoke or dismantle it. Humility always destroys the killer of comparison because it disarms any power of retaliation. Comparison always wants to exalt itself but humility bows low and lets others be exalted. It is just like killing with kindness but honoring with humility!

Competition Is for Orphans

> *Comparison fuels the fire of ungodly competition.*

I have always been a competitive person. I grew up in a family that loved to play games, but more than that, we loved to win. The winner was always the hero—someone to be respected and revered. I quickly learned that no one liked the loser, so I made sure that I was always a winner.

Because of this mindset, I've always struggled with needing to be the "best" in the room. I believed the lie that the most powerful person was the most gifted, talented or educated person. All of this stems from comparison because the only way to be a "winner" is to measure yourself up to others. Unfortunately, this is too often the case amongst young leaders.

While we are all trying to go after what God has called us to do, it can be tempting to compete with others around us. The problem with this mentality is that it is birthed in an orphan spirit. An orphan spirit is a spirit that knows nothing of inheritance and plenty.

Think of it like this: an orphan is a child who has no parents. Therefore, that child must fight for him or herself. Everything they have, they receive because they themselves have fought for it. But what if, one day, a King ordered that orphan child to be taken to the palace and adopted? At once, the child would be bathed and clothed in royal garments—transformed completely!

The only problem is that the child might look different outwardly, but inwardly, that child is still and orphan. When at the dinner table, you might see the child hiding food in their pockets out of fear that they won't have another meal later or eating too quickly in fear of it being stolen by one of the other kids. For this child to become royalty, they must lose their old mindsets and realize that there is more than enough for them and all the other children in the King's house.

Young leaders who feel the need to compete don't realize that there is more than enough for them and their brothers and sisters in Christ.

When we kill the issue of comparison, there is no need to compete with those around us. Instead, we can celebrate with one another's wins!

When an orphan sees their sibling get blessed, they get jealous and critical because they believe that's one less blessing for them

When a child of God sees their sibling get blessed, they celebrate because they know the same Father who blessed their sibling is the same Father who will bless them!

How to Beat Comparison

I believe that if Joseph had used wisdom in sharing his dreams, he could have avoided what came next. Did God, in His sovereignty, use this situation to get him where He wanted Joseph to end up? Of course! Nothing we do in the Kingdom is ever wasted because God can make beautiful things out of ugly situations. However, just as I missed out on an incredible friendship during my time at CFNI, I believe Joseph could have avoided great pain by serving his brothers in humility.

So how can we walk in humility and dismantle this killer? Here are some ways we as young leaders can say "YES" to humility. This will result in living a comparison-free life, free from criticism and competition.

DISCOVER YOUR IDENTITY

You will never stop comparing yourself with others until your start discovering who you really are. I remember growing up with a friend of mine who always had the coolest stuff. His room was amazing and always made me want to redo mine to look just as cool as his. I made a hobby of everything he loved in hopes that I would be as awesome as him someday, however, I was always miserable and never felt like I had enough. It was not until I realized who *I* was and who God called *me* to be that I started living in joy and contentment. Knowing who you are starts with knowing who you belong to. You just so happen to belong to a God, who loves, enjoys, protects, covers and provides for you no matter what. Stay grounded in your identity and stop comparing yourself with someone you were never meant to be!

DESTROY YOUR DISTRACTIONS

Whether it is through social media, magazines, entertainment, pop culture, or whatever tool you use to compare yourself with others—JUST STOP! Comparison is a deadly disease that has no mercy and cannot be negotiated with. Get rid of the triggers that cause you to compare and start looking at Jesus. Focus on the call He has given you and pursue that. Stop trying to be something you are not and grow in who God has made you to be. There will always be haters, but you do not have to be one of them. Love yourself and love the path God has placed in front of you. You can never be YOU if you are always trying to be someone else.

PRACTICE HUMILITY

Jesus tells us in Luke 14 to sit at the "lowest seat of the table" whenever we are at a dinner party. In other words, always assume the position of a servant. This does not mean that you have a lowly view of yourself and walk around with your head hanging. Knowing who you are in Christ solidifies your identity as a prince or a princess of the Kingdom, but good princes and princesses have no problem serving others. They know that their authority has been given to them so that they can serve effectively. Wherever you go, get low. Do not pursue notoriety or publicity. Serve well and let God exalt you in due time. He knows where to find you!

PREFER OTHERS

The best way to avoid invoking comparison in others is to constantly build others up. Honor dismantles competition. A person who is secure in who they are feels no need to put others down, instead they make a practice of building others up putting others first. Instead of gloating in your calling and favor, exalt others. Draw attention to those around you. Bless those who curse you and live a lifestyle of honor, even when they do not deserve it. That is not your problem—YOU ARE!

PRAY CONSTANTLY

Prayerlessness is always a product of pride. Make sure that you ask the Holy Spirit for humility and honor to walk out your call with dignity and integrity. Deal with any issues of comparison together. Ask forgiveness of those whom you have compared yourself to and renew your mind with the truth of God's word.

Activation:

Do you struggle with comparison? Have you done a good job of being a servant-leader instead of being arrogant with the call on your life? Ask the Lord to show you if you have compared or competed with others and ask Him how to walk in wisdom and humility as a leader!

Prayer:

God, I repent of my attitude of comparison. I recognize that in You I have all things and that comparison is a form of ungratefulness for all that You have given me. Forgive me and teach me how to serve like Jesus served.

8

the pit

Let's pick back up with the story of Joseph.

Then his brothers went to feed their father's flock in Shechem. And Israel said to Joseph, "Are not your brothers feeding the flock in Shechem? Come, I will send you to them." So he said to him, "Here I am."

Then he said to him, "Please go and see if it is well with your brothers and well with the flocks, and bring back word to me." So he sent him out of the Valley of Hebron, and he went to Shechem.

Now a certain man found him, and there he was, wandering in the field. And the man asked him, saying, "What are you seeking?"

So he said, "I am seeking my brothers. Please tell me where they are feeding their flocks."

And the man said, "They have departed from here, for I heard them say, 'Let us go to Dothan.'" So Joseph went after his brothers and found them in Dothan.

Now when they saw him afar off, even before he came near them, they conspired against him to kill him. Then they said to one another, "Look, this dreamer is coming! Come therefore, let us now kill him and cast him into some pit; and we shall say, 'Some wild beast has devoured him.' We shall see what will become of his dreams!"

But Reuben heard it, and he delivered him out of their hands, and said, "Let us not kill him." And Reuben said to them, "Shed no blood, but cast him into this pit which is in the wilderness, and do not lay a hand on him"—that he might deliver him out of their hands, and bring him back to his father.

So it came to pass, when Joseph had come to his brothers, that they stripped Joseph of his tunic, the tunic of many colors that was on him. Then they took him and cast him into a pit. And the pit was empty; there was no water in it.
Genesis 36:12–24

The Killer's Plot

Ah, the pit. The place we must all face at least once in our lives, but unfortunately, the honest truth is that we will probably face it far more than once. If you are called to a life of divine impact, I can guarantee you that there will be many "pit stops" along the way, but in this chapter we will focus our attention on the first of two that are outlined in the text.

The first "pit stop" that Joseph makes is quite a personal one. I'd like to make a distinction between the first and second "pit" that Joseph experiences in his journey as a young leader:

The Pit is the place of loss, due to the call on your life.

Because you have made up your mind about who you are going to be, the Pit is a place you will be thrown into outside of your control. It is the place of loneliness, betrayal, loss of relationships, heartache, and separation.

Joseph has just finished sharing his dreams with his brothers and they're not so "on board" with them as he is. They are already struggling internally with comparison, competition and conviction. If I *yes.*

could imagine what was going on in their heads, it would probably sound something like this:

"Who does this kid think he is? He thinks HE'S going to be the one to make something of his life? And WE ARE going to bow down to HIM? WE ARE the ones that have been working and toiling for our father all these years. No, this spoiled, little brat is not going ANYWHERE . . . in fact, we are going to make sure that he does not make it out of this family alive!"

In an instant, the Killer of Comparison strategizes a plan of action. The similar story of Cain and Abel fades into a forgotten memory as Joseph's brothers continue the Killer's legacy and arrange for Joseph's murder. This will be the end of his dreams, his destiny; they would make sure of it.

Let me remind you about the account in Genesis 4. As stated earlier, Cain sees the favor and blessing upon the life of his brother, Abel, and decides that he simply cannot bear the idea that his brother has a purpose. After both having had provided God with a sacrifice, Yahweh accepted Abel's offering but rejected Cain's. As soon as he looked over at his brother's success, Cain's issue with comparison turns into action and in a moment, Cain goes down in history as the first murderer by spilling the blood of his brother.

Can you see a thread here? In an instant, what started as a heart issue turns into a plan of action to destroy the competition! This is how comparison works, it crushes its prey and consumes the predator!

Throw Him Away

After a long deliberation of how they would go about destroying their brother, almost everyone decided that it was best to kill him. The ancient thirst for blood that would lead straight to the line of Cain was invoked in their hearts until one of them spoke up.

"Let's not kill him. Let his blood not be on our hands. If he dies in the pit, so be it, but let not our souls pay for the price of his death!"

Reuben, one of Joseph's brothers, advocates on his behalf and fights for his life.

They all agreed, at least there was *some* fear of God in their hearts. They ambushed Joseph and bound his hands and feet. There was no

86

way that he could overpower all of them, he was outnumbered, and they were too strong. He struggled and fought but, as he looked at the faces of the men who had ambushed him, he started to give up. His heart began to break as he realized what was happening to him and who was actually taking him captive.

His brothers were perplexed by the lack of struggle. They laughed with joy and mocked him until they looked down at the face of their brother. They watched as tears began to stream down his cheeks, but it was too late. Hatred had taken over their hearts and in their minds Joseph, was no longer considered their brother.

Betrayal

The moment of betrayal is an incredibly deep wound. I am sure we all have experienced betrayal to some degree in our lives, but to be betrayed by your own blood is another thing altogether.

Being in ministry, especially in a pastoral role, I have suffered betrayal many times. Whether it be by the people I serve, fellow staff members, or leaders that I have submitted to, betrayal never feels good. Being betrayed by someone you work with hurts. Being betrayed by someone you do ministry with hurts even more but, there is nothing more painful than being betrayed by your own blood.

A situation in my own family occurred around the time I was leaving for Bible school that devastated us. For protection and confidentiality, I will refrain from sharing the details of it all, but I can tell you that, aside from losing dad, it was one of the most difficult times my family ever had to walk through. When all of this happened and the truth came out, not only did we discover that we had been lied to and deceived for years but we were standing on the other side of a dividing line between two families. The confrontation was horrible and felt like a bomb had exploded with pieces of our hearts flying everywhere.

In some ways it seemed like we had become outcasts for standing for the truth and had lost everything because of it. The deepest hurt came from the fact that we felt alienated from our own family.

All in all, both sides were probably experiencing the same feelings of isolation and division. The enemy is a master of breaking in and dividing loved ones by convincing them that they are better off alone than together. He breaks down our connections with each other through lies and destroys the unity that God intended for families. I am glad to say that God is in the business of restoration and I am watching Him work, even years later. The process of forgiveness and reconciliation is in full effect and I am overjoyed at what God is doing with such a messy situation, yet I must say that it was one of the most difficult times we have ever had to walk through.

Betrayal is a deep wound. Not only does it include deception, but at some level it almost seems to involve thievery. Think about how you would feel if you were walking to your car, only to realize that someone had broken into it the night before and stolen everything inside. The only difference is betrayal means the person who robbed you was your next-door neighbor or your best friend. It is a feeling that cannot be fully explained in words, but one thing is for certain; it is a feeling that I would not wish upon anyone.

The Sting of Separation

What Joseph may not have understood was that, although it came in the form of betrayal, God was ultimately separating him from his surroundings. And sometimes, God will use the most painful way to separate us from our current situations so he can move us closer to our calling.

The word "consecration" seems to be a bit outdated in our current culture, but it is important that I educate you on the term because, if you are called to be a young leader, you must say "YES" to a life of consecration. Consequently, this means separation.

Although we will talk more about this in the next chapter, we must realize that sometimes the process to our promise will only come through pain. Do you remember feeling "growing pains" as a child? You could be lying in bed at night and all of a sudden, the sense of stretching and movement would cause pain throughout your entire body. It was never a pleasant sensation, but it was necessary for your body to grow.

The sting of separation is always a painful one, but it leads us to the place of consecration to God. As young leaders, we must be ready to experience loss for the gain of our lives in Christ.

Guarding Your Heart Against Betrayal

As we walk out the purpose for our lives, we will undoubtedly face times like these. Whether it has happened to you or not, I can assure you that if you work with people, you will face the sting of betrayal. It is almost impossible to prepare your heart for a situation like this because, to be in true community, we must be trusting and vulnerable with others. This means taking the risk of being hurt.

However, there are healthy ways to guard your heart. You can fix your eyes on Jesus to be the true, faithful friend that you need when it seems like you have no others.

Although it was painful, Joseph accepted the place of separation. Here are a couple of ways you too can say "YES" to consecration, even when betrayal stands before you.

TRUST IN GOD WHO MAKES A WAY

Joseph's brothers took him and threw him into a pit. They had intended to kill him, but thankfully Joseph had an advocate in his brother, Reuben. I am fully convinced that this was the sovereign work of God to protect Joseph and his destiny. Even when the enemy had plotted to steal, kill and destroy him, God was coming to give life and life more abundantly (John 10:10).

First and foremost, we must understand that no matter what situation comes our way, no weapon that is formed against us will be able to prosper (Isa. 54:17). The word prosper in the Hebrew is *tsâlêach*, which means "to be profitable" or "to be successful." Notice what it DOES NOT say. It does not tell us that no *weapons* will be formed against us. You had better believe that living out your purpose will tick off some devils and they will do anything, even throw you in the pit of betrayal, to wage war upon your calling. Look at the promise: "No weapon formed against you *will be able to prosper!*" God always has a man on the inside. Even if He has to use your enemies, God will make sure that you are not destroyed and that no plan of the enemy succeeds. Look at the promises Paul tells us we have:

"We are hard-pressed on every side, yet not crushed; we are perplexed, but not in despair; persecuted, but not forsaken; struck down, but not destroyed."
2 Corinthians 4:8–9

"What shall we say then? If God is for us, then who can be against us?"
Romans 8:31

I am reminded of the story of Lot and his family in Genesis 19. Even in the darkest of circumstances, God still found and rescued His own! You can rest assured that no matter who is against you, God is FOR you!

DON'T BE SURPRISED WHEN FRIENDS TURN TO FOES

"We shall see what will become of his dreams!"

Can you imagine this moment? Maybe you have already lived through something similar, but either way, it is a situation that no man or woman wishes to be in. It looks something like this: the very people who have claimed to be your family are now the ones who are throwing you into the pit of despair to be left for dead. Ouch!

Joseph, bruised and battered, lies at the bottom of the pit and weeps himself into the dust. All he ever wanted was to serve the Lord. All he ever dreamt of was making an impact. He was not trying to disqualify his brothers! His heart was never to come off as arrogant or prideful. He was simply sharing his dreams with the people he loved. Why did they not understand? How could they do this to him?

As you walk your calling out in front of others, you may find yourself in a place where the people who are closest to you become the ones who hurt you the most. You may have shared the deepest parts of your dreams and passions with them and instead of joining with you; they turn around and throw you in a pit.

Knowing that this is a possibility should not keep you from trusting others or getting close to friends and family. As I stated earlier, guarding your heart is not putting up walls, it is keeping your hope in Jesus. Knowing that sometimes the people we expect to carry us let us down reminds us that there is no one who is perfect, only Jesus.

When you find yourself in a pit, all seems lost and everyone around you has abandoned you, the God who never leaves you is right by your side. He has not forgotten your future; in fact, He commands your destiny.

I love the lyrics written by Stuart Townend in the last verse of his hymn, "In Christ Alone":

> *"No guilt in life, no fear in death*
> *This is the power of Christ in me*
> *From life's first cry to final breath*
> *Jesus commands my destiny.*
> *No power of hell, no scheme of man*
> *Could ever pluck me from His hand*
> *Till He returns or calls me home*
> *Here in the power of Christ I stand."*

LIVE TO PLEASE GOD, NOT PEOPLE

Not everyone is going to partner with you in the call of God on your life or understand the expression of that call. Because of this, the people that you have allowed to hold your heart can be the very ones who crush it. Do you remember Jesus as He rode the donkey into Jerusalem? The same crowd that cheered, "Hosanna" was the same crowd that, only days later, chanted, "Crucify him!"

One of my favorite quotes from Bill Johnson is, "If you live by the praises of men you will die by their criticisms." Human nature is truly fickle. In a moment, the people who praised you can become the same people who persecute you and throw you in a pit. Instead of lifting you up, they work to make you feel disqualified in your dream and cause you to question whether or not your dream is even attainable.

However, deep the hurt may be, there is one truth that we must hold onto: *God is the God of the pit.*

91

In the moments of our lives that we feel disqualified from our calling, our God is the One who remains sovereign over all. The pit is necessary because without the pit, our dreams and our destinies can be so mistakenly placed in the hands of the people around us. Our brothers, our fathers, our mothers, and our pastors, we look to them to validate the call on our lives instead of the Giver of the call. We take comfort in their affirmation, trusting that if *they* believe in this calling of ours, maybe we are not failures after all.

But therein lies the problem. They never gave you the call, and the call does not belong to them.

Because the Giver of the call is jealous of the called, the pit is an absolute necessity.

You see, while Joseph wept himself into the dust, the Lord was teaching him a very important lesson: the God who formed man from the dust needed no assistance from the dust to bring forth destiny. He simply needed dust.

All He Needs Is You

The truth is that God will sometimes allow those whom He has called to be thrown into the pit of despair to show them that HE ALONE is Lord over their call. You do not need someone else to validate you to be able to do what GOD called you to do. You do not need the right connections, the big promotion, the best strategies, all you need is the One who called you because He promises to be faithful to complete it (Phil. 1:6).

Here is the key: in the midst of the turmoil, God is calling us to trust in His promises. At the bottom of the pit we are reminded that God simply breathed upon dust and formed man. He did not need help then, and He does not need help now. When God speaks, it is fact. A leader must believe in spite of what he does not see, but only what he knows to be true. At the end of the day, the only truth that will stand is the truth that God has declared!

Smith Wigglesworth said it best,

> *"I am not moved by what I see. I am not moved by what I feel.*
> *I am only moved by what I believe."*

Activation:

Do you feel like you are in a spiritual pit? Have you lost friends, loved ones or followers? Are you alone and frustrated? Remember that God is forming you to be the very leader that you are called to be. Progress hardly comes without pain; weeping endures for the night, but joy comes in the morning!

Prayer:

God, it feels like I am in the pit. Sometimes I wonder where You are, but today I choose to trust that You are Lord over the pit. Encourage my heart and strengthen my faith in You so that I can stand firm in my resolve to follow You.

9

the loneliness of leadership

There is a great Afghani proverb on leadership that says, "If you think you are leading and no one is following, you are just taking a walk."

It takes a lot of courage, strength, and wisdom to be a leader. Leaders have always fascinated the human race. We study their lives, their behavior, and their legacies. We write books about them and make monuments to them. We even, in some cases, set holidays aside to celebrate them! Leaders make hard decisions that the average person runs from. They stand up when no one else around them is willing to take a stand. Ultimately, we follow them because we admire the courage it takes for them to do the things we could only dream of doing.

Although seemingly glamorous, the road to becoming a successful leader is far from it. I believe leaders are formed and molded through the fires of life's tests, yet I believe that ultimately, the call and anointing of God is the anchor that keeps effective leaders standing strong and moving forward. The number of leaders who persevere through trying times are few, but those who lay down their lives for the sake of others pave the way for great accomplishments that will never be forgotten.

A leader is like the captain of the football team. He is the first to show up and the last to leave. He studies plays while the rest of the team is out partying. He eats, sleeps, and breathes the game. Internally, he is driven by a resolve to win that burns deep within his heart. It almost seems as if his entire life depends on the failure or success of his goal. A natural leader steps up to inspire the rest of his team and can be identified without any title or elevated position. It is something *inside* of him that draws out determination in others.

Just the other day, I was watching the classic movie *We Were Soldiers* and I was reminded of how influential a strong leader can be. Mel Gibson plays the character of Colonel Moore, the leader of a battalion sent into one of the most intense battles of the Vietnam War. It is an incredible movie, but one part had the greatest impact on me.

The scene takes place right before the battalion is sent out to battle. Colonel Moore gathers his soldiers together and makes a speech to inspire his men to fight valiantly. He approaches the podium and stands before his soldiers and their wives. Much to their surprise, Moore makes no grandiose claims or promises of victory. Instead, he tells his men that he *cannot* promise that they will all make it out alive, however, there is one thing that they could count on: no matter what happened on the battlefield, good or bad, his men would be able to trust him to be a strong leader. He would be the first on the ground and the last to leave. He would lead them into battle and carry back the wounded. He assured them that even if they faced defeat, he would never back down from his responsibility to lead them, and would stand strong when everyone else around him might fall.

Colonel Moore showed that being a leader means stepping up and venturing into difficult situations, which prepares the way for others to succeed. By looking at the life of Joseph, we can see this call of leadership from the very beginning. He may not have fully known what he was getting himself into, but he would soon learn that answering the call meant walking through the fires of testing.

So far, we have identified several keys from Joseph's journey that can help us move forward in leadership. Each one brings a level of understanding and revelation to what our process may look like, as we too say, "YES" to our purpose. However, the lesson that we are about to learn is not only incredibly important, it is often times incredibly painful. This lesson is found in the "pit of loneliness." As much as I hate to say it, there is absolutely no way of avoiding seasons of loneliness if one is called to lead. A life lived for God will, without a doubt, find itself in lonely places.

Hear me before you read any further; this chapter was NOT written to depress you and it was NOT written to get you to believe that, as a leader, you are supposed to be a "lone ranger" and reject people. That could not be farther from the truth! However, I must share with you the realities of what comes along with the call to lead, even when it is not fun!

Joseph's Journey Through Loneliness

Let's pick up with Joseph's story. He has just been thrown into a pit, not to mention, by his own brothers. He has been betrayed, abandoned and is now completely and utterly alone.

> *"And they took him and threw him into a pit. The pit was **empty**; there was **no water** in it."*
> *Genesis 37:24*

I find it very interesting that the writer of the story takes the time to tell us that the pit was "empty and without water." It could have been a simple description of the pit, letting the reader know that it was not a well filled with water in which he might drown. Maybe the writer did not even think twice about what he was writing. However, I find it intriguing that the pit was described as "empty" and "without water" and I believe there is a deeper revelation that God desires for us to see, if we ask.

From the moment Joseph was born, he was a leader. The coat of many colors set him apart from his brothers and one could speculate that Joseph experienced loneliness quite often. We know that his brothers hated him. Obviously, his dad loved him, but in the accounts of his 'dream-sharing,' his father also takes part in the ridicule and persecution. I think it is safe to assume that Joseph spent time alone, but nothing he had experienced up until now compared to the pit.

I believe Joseph made some real mistakes as a young leader, some of which we have already discussed, however, it is undeniable that Joseph's life irritated those around him who struggled with his call and his purpose. Now, it had led him to the loneliest place of his life.

The pit was different. Trapping him with rejection and abandonment, the pit introduced Joseph to loneliness so bitter that it would change his life forever. I believe that in this pit lies a secret to understanding the seasons of loneliness that we, as young leaders, will walk through. By looking deeper at its attributes, we can truly see that the pit can leave us "empty" and "without water."

Empty

In the pit, we can find ourselves not only alone but feeling incredibly empty. The reason emptiness creeps in with loneliness is because we begin to lose the vision of our destinies.

When you are thrown in the pit, all you can see are walls around you. For visionaries, this becomes crippling. Proverbs 29:18 tells us that without vision, people perish. The pit forces us to deal with the possibility that our destinies have been cut off from us and we are now powerless, and unable to get back on track.

As a native New Yorker, New York City was always one of my favorite places to visit. I grew up on Long Island, so to get into the city, all I had to do was hop on the Long Island Rail Road and take the train right into Penn Station. Even as a "born and raised" New Yorker, the city is completely overwhelming. Altogether, the NYC area is about 468 square miles, and in 2012 it was estimated to have a population of over 8.3 million people. Standing on the street in the middle of Times Square gives you a sense of how small you are, and how big the city really is.

However, if you get on an airplane and fly above the city, you can see with an entirely new perspective. Through the window, you are able to see the city in all of its glory. You have to get high enough because the city is so large, but once you see it from that perspective, mapping out the city is much easier than standing in the middle of the city on ground level.

Being in the pit is like being a tourist, standing on the street in the middle Times Square. The sheer magnitude of the city and its mystery is so overwhelming that many feel the urge to quit before they even start. You cannot see beyond the towering buildings and lights to even know where you are, and a sense of emptiness can begin to fill your heart as you realize that there is no way you could possibly make it.

Guard against emptiness while in the season of the pit.

Remember that it is only a season, and God is bringing breakthrough that will take you to higher perspectives to see the big picture and remind you of your purpose.

Without Water

Another feeling you can experience in the pit is spiritual dryness and dehydration. Not only are you alone and empty, but you realize that there is nothing around you to bring you life and refreshment; the relationships that you once leaned on are now gone and the vision you once pursued now seems hopeless. All the while, God feels absent. Your frustration with Him leads to a rejection of prayer and reading of the Word, and you begin to find yourself dying of thirst. The pit is a dry and waterless place, and it strips you of any spiritual hydration that you are accustomed to.

Guard against spiritual dryness in the season of the pit.

It may be waterless, but the Bible tells us that inside of us are rivers of living water (see John 7:38). Your season may not offer you hydration but, your Source never lacks in refreshing water for your soul.

My Struggle with Loneliness

Loneliness has always been something I have always dealt with, even before I started walking with the Lord. I have never been the type of person who loves to be with big groups. Parties always seemed shallow to me, and there is nothing I hate more than small talk. Instead of having lots of 'acquaintances,' I have always prioritized having a small number of deep relationships. Because 'being known' is such a big deal to me, it is important that I have friends who have seen the real "Jared" and accept and understand me. I also have a short fuse, and often need to get away to recharge by being alone.

Growing up, being in large groups always made me feel like the odd one out. It seemed like I just did not fit anywhere. Even when I was with my friends, something was always off. This was magnified one hundred times when I really started walking with the Lord. Not only did I *feel* like I did not fit, I really *DID NOT* fit.

After I had my encounter with God, I decided that my life needed changing. Because of this, I began to lose all of my friends. My band-mates did not agree with my decision to leave the band to pursue ministry and became angry with me. They felt as if I had betrayed them and let them down. My other friends did not understand why I did not want to partake in the same activities that I was once a part of. Because they did not know how to handle this, it was easier for them to just walk away from me all together. I found myself growing in leadership, but lacking in friendships. It was if I had been thrust into the pit of loneliness, and I had no control over it!

The Lord began to show me that the call to leadership is a call to be "other than."

To make a difference, you must BE different.

To be *different,* sometimes you must be separated from those around you to allow God to form you into what He is calling you to be.

Once again, I am not saying that being a leader is an excuse to walk away from all of your friends because of your call. I am describing the seasons of our lives when it feels like we have no control over a lack of relationships and a sense of loneliness. Do not confuse this with an isolating spirit that attempts to cut you off from healthy community and separate you through arrogance and pride!

The Leader's Climb

Stepping up to be a leader is not an easy task. Often times, leadership is a lonely place. Just a few days ago, I was out with one of the student interns of Youth Church and he began to express his frustration with the loneliness he was experiencing. It seemed as if he had lost all of his friends; everyone had abandoned and rejected him. He was confused because he had been passionately pursuing the Lord. It seemed like he was doing everything right, so why was everyone leaving him? Why was it so lonely?

When you are called to be a leader, it is as if you are answering the call to climb a mountain. At the beginning of the voyage, the climb seems easy. Lots of people surround the base and admire its grandness and size, however, the higher the climb, the rockier the terrain. The going gets tough and is not meant for everyone. Because of this level of difficulty, only the strong and determined climbers continue upward. The crowd gets smaller and so does the square footage on the mountain. As it stretches to the heavens, the mountain offers less and less footing. There are many who can admire the mountain but there are few who can scale it to the top. The peak is reserved for the select few who are willing to risk it all; it is the mountain's reward for the man or woman brave enough to climb higher, even if it means doing it alone.

Leaders are called climb to the peak of the mountain, to live from a higher level. A leader needs this elevated perspective to lead effectively. People follow them because they can see things that people on the ground cannot. Just like the illustration of NYC, higher perspective means greater vision. They are willing to brave the terrain that no one else is willing to endure, all for the sake of advancing others.

An elevated position does not mean that a leader is better than their followers are; in fact, it is the exact opposite.

The higher the call, the more the leader must serve.

A higher position means a higher perspective, and a higher perspective means a higher responsibility to look out for others. This is where a servant's heart comes in. Leaders climb the mountain not to elevate *themselves*, but to get *others* to a higher level. They make trails and roadways so that those who follow them will be able to climb with ease. They explore unchartered territory and create maps. They are forerunners, pioneers who live their lives to open up possibilities for others. Sometimes, this means going the journey alone. Why? Well, not everyone wants to lay down their lives for others.

The Risk of Rough Terrain

I was watching a documentary the other day on mountain climbing called *The Summit*. It showed a group of people who attempted to climb K2, the world's second largest peak. Although smaller than Mt. Everest, K2 is believed to be the most dangerous mountain on earth. It is said that some three hundred climbers have attempted to reach the top, and over eighty-five have lost their lives trying.

Some people view mountain climbers as those who just want to gloat; they are arrogant, adrenaline junkies who do it all for the notoriety. As I watched this documentary, I realized that it could not be farther from the truth. The documentary team spent hours interviewing numerous climbers who had scaled multiple peaks. While watching these interviews, I noticed something that astonished me: every climber seemed to have an inner resolve to get to the top of these mountains, not simply for public notoriety. They had a personal ambition to discover unchartered territory and put their bodies to the ultimate test. They did not care about what other people thought about them; they did not even seem bothered by the risks. *They were motivated to do something that had never been done before.*

One of the climbers who really impressed me was the first of his country to summit K2. He could not have been more proud to have paved the way for his nation and watch his country's flag fly with all the others. What a moment of pride and honor!

This man inspired me and got me thinking: this is the call to leadership. We must be motivated to put everything on the line to reach places that seem unreachable, and live to tell about it. Our passion to climb must come from an inner resolve to advance. Not simply for us, but for the ones we pave the way for. Everything we do must be done keeping in mind people who we will share our stories with. They may have never dreamt of reaching the heights we have reached, but our progress and our process may be the very inspiration they needed to take one step higher and journey one step deeper into their own purpose.

Living your life for the sake of others is a sacrifice, and this kind of sacrifice is a high risk. Climbing a mountain is risky business. You could slip and fall. You could get lost. You could lose consciousness due to the high altitudes. There are many dangers in trailblazing, but a leader knows that at the end of the day, people are worth the risk. This is incredibly important for young leaders to understand. When we are young, we can fall into the trap that leads us to believe that leadership is about people serving us. It is the opposite. We must serve others. Loving people, not power, is what matters and must be our motivation.

Many might think that Joseph took the risk when he shared his dreams with his brothers. I believe that there was a level of risk in that decision, but not enough risk to truly pave the way for others to move forward. No, the risk was not something he could choose. The risk had to be chosen for him.

That risk was submitting to the pit of loneliness.

Facing Loneliness

We will see later on in Joseph's life how this pit prepared him for the trials that would soon face him. But, what we can tell so far from his story is that there will be seasons of loneliness as we walk the path that God has set before us.

Even when all of his brothers abandoned him and his father believed him to be dead, Joseph was never alone. The *God of the Pit* was right there with him.

We all were created for relationships. In the Garden of Eden, God looked upon man (before He had created woman) and made a powerful statement:

"It is not good for man to be alone."
(Gen 2:18)

God created us with a hole in our hearts that He chose not to fill. He created Eve as a helpmate and revealed to us our design for human relationships. It is of utmost importance to realize that we NEED people in our lives, and that need is not unhealthy unless it takes God's place.

Yet, there will be times when the option of having these types of relationships does not exist. It will feel like you have been thrown into a pit and are powerless, unable to connect with people around you.

> *To grow from seasons of loneliness, we must turn*
> *"loneliness" into "aloneness."*

One of the most important lessons I have ever learned was the lesson of 'aloneness.' As a leader, you will not be able to avoid seasons of loneliness. Some will experience this more than others, but I can assure that every leader must walk through seasons of the pit. To be victorious in the midst of this season, you must learn to transform loneliness into aloneness.

Webster's Dictionary defines loneliness as "sadness that comes from being apart from other people." It defines aloneness as "being separated from others." One has a negative connotation, while the other is intentional.

> *You may not be able to control the season of the pit,*
> *but you can control what you do while you're in it.*

I can tell you that I am currently in one of the loneliest seasons of my life, yet here I am, writing this book and this very chapter on this very subject to encourage you with my story. Taking what the enemy used for evil and using it for good is the ultimate victory.

You have a choice to live as a victim or a victor. Leaders always view themselves as victors. As long as you hold to the perception that you are a victim of your season, you will walk around defeated and depressed. Nothing good will come out of your experiences, because you are not focused on the "good things" that God causes to come together from your bad situation. Victims live affected and ruled by their circumstances, feeling powerless. They often complain and grumble instead of conquer and grow.

Take control of your loneliness and get intentional with it. It is in this season that God calls us to Himself and grows us in intimacy with Him that could never be possible when surrounded by friends and family. Do not allow the enemy to fill your mind with depressing thoughts. Immerse yourself in the Word and renew your mind. Make use of your season, and find God's purpose in it. The truth is that you are NEVER alone. Deuteronomy 31:6 tells us that God will never leave us and never forsake us. Take hold of the truth and walk in victory, even when it feels like no one is around to see it.

To overcome loneliness, you must learn to have a friend in Jesus.

After being in the pit, Joseph's brothers sold him into slavery, and not just any kind slavery. He was sold into the possession of the Egyptians, a godless nation far from his home. Now, Joseph was surrounded with people but, his loneliness only seemed to increase.

There will be times in your journey when you are in the midst of lots of people and still feel like an alien in a foreign land, lost in a sea of faces. Loneliness is at its worst when it is in the midst of company. Whether it is in a social setting, the workplace, your ministry, or even your family, just because there are people in your life does not mean that you are always connected to them in a life-giving way. This can be the most hurtful form of loneliness. There is only one way to keep your heart from bitterness and frustration with those around you in the place of "lonely company."

I want to encourage you with the words of an old hymn, penned by Joseph M. Scriven:

> What a Friend we have in Jesus,
> all our sins and griefs to bear!
> What a privilege to carry
> everything to God in prayer!
>
> O what peace we often forfeit,
> O what needless pain we bear,
> All because we do not carry
> everything to God in prayer.
>
> Have we trials and temptations?

Is there trouble anywhere?
We should never be discouraged;
take it to the Lord in prayer.

Can we find a friend so faithful
who will all our sorrows share?
Jesus knows our every weakness;
take it to the Lord in prayer.
Are we weak and heavy laden,
cumbered with a load of care?

Precious Savior, still our refuge,
take it to the Lord in prayer.
Do your friends despise, forsake you?
Take it to the Lord in prayer!
In His arms He'll take and shield you;
you will find a solace there.
Blessed Savior, Thou hast promised
Thou wilt all our burdens bear

May we ever, Lord, be bringing
all to Thee in earnest prayer.

Soon in glory bright unclouded
there will be no need for prayer

Rapture, praise and endless worship
will be our sweet portion there.
(emphasis added)

Oh, what a friend we have in Jesus. Not only are we never alone, Jesus is a friend that sticks closer than a brother. He is our refuge and our strength, an ever-present help in time of need (see Psalm 46).

In the moments when you feel isolated in a crowd of people, remember the friend you have in Jesus. Like the hymn so beautifully tells us, take it to the Lord in prayer. Let Him carry the burden and the pain. Allow Jesus to share in your grief and comfort you with His precious Holy Spirit.

Will You Keep Climbing?

As I watched that documentary on K2, the cameras showed the highest peak of the mountain. It was evident that with rockier and steeper ground, the climb promises to be physically taxing. The higher altitude causes oxygen levels to become scarce and mental functions become more difficult to carry out. Each step upward declares that there is no turning back. So the question posed to you is: will you keep climbing?

The truth is, there are few who are willing to press on, but for those who do there is a great reward waiting at the top of the mountain:

> *"I press on toward the goal to win the prize for which God has called me upward in Christ Jesus."*
> *Philippians 3:14*

I can honestly say that even though the seasons of loneliness are painful, there is always purpose in the pain. God has always proved Himself faithful to me and has used all of the times I felt were wasted to lead and inspire others to keep moving forward.

You cannot fail if you do not quit.

We all desire to hear the words, "Well done, My good and faithful servant" at the end of our lives. Notice Jesus says "faithful servant." God is looking for those who will stay faithful in the fight and persevere through the pit.

There will be so many opportunities to quit. All the enemy wants to do is to get you to walk away from the call by showing you how difficult it is going to be. Do not fall for his tricks. The Devil is a liar; that is all he can do. Even a half-truth is a lie, and by showing you the difficulty of the season, he only shares a small portion of the journey God desires to take you on.

God's purpose for you is so great and so exciting, yet there are times when we must walk through pain to develop our story and minister to those who need someone who can understand. Look at what Paul writes to us in 2 Corinthians:

> *Blessed be the God and Father of our Lord Jesus Christ, the Father of mercies and God of all comfort, who comforts us in all our tribulation,* ***that we may be able to comfort those who are in any trouble, with the comfort with which we ourselves are comforted by God.***
> *2 Corinthians 1:3–4 (emphasis added)*

Do not allow the enemy to give you tunnel vision. Ask God to reveal the big picture to you. In the season of the pit, the same comfort that you receive from God will be the comfort that you can give to others and help them find their purpose.

You Are Not Alone

This is the loneliness found in the life of a leader. You may have started to climb with groups of people around you, but the higher you climbed, the less company you now find yourself in. It does not make you better than them, but it does define you as a leader, and sets you apart.

Remember this: you are never alone. Not every season will be this way. God will lead you into seasons where He will surround you with people who can encourage and comfort you, but before you can experience those things from people, you must first experience them from the Holy Spirit. HE must be your source. This lesson will keep you grounded like a foundation built upon the rock. You will not blow away in the wind nor be swept away by the waves. The house built upon Jesus will never fail and Jesus will never let you down!

<u>*Activation:*</u>

Loneliness is a huge part of being a leader. To be a leader means to go places where others have not gone before. To do this success-fully, you will need the comfort and companionship of the Holy Spirit. Take some time to ask the Lord for courage as you venture into new territory!

<u>*Prayer:*</u>

God, in my loneliness I trust that You are with me. I resolve to not back down from the climb that You have set in front of me. Give me the strength and the courage to walk through times where it feels like no one else is around me. Increase my awareness of Your Holy Spirit in me and comfort me in my times of need.

10

the power of promotion

One of my favorite things to do is to work out. I love lifting weights. Growing up, I was not very athletic. I was fast and lean, but short and lacking in fine motor skills. I was much more interested in music, so I kept my distance from sports, however, when I got to college, I realized that the short, skinny white kid was NOT what I envisioned for my future, so I started working out with my friend Mike. Mike was huge. His biceps were the size of my legs. Working out with him was a great motivator because every day that we worked out, I had a goal to reach just by looking at him. My competitive nature would not let this guy out-lift me, no matter how much bigger than me he was.

In the course of the first three months, I gained about 15 pounds of muscle. I ate constantly and lifted heavy weights so that I could pack on more and more muscle mass. The transformation was astounding. People saw me in the gym and did a double take. They could not believe that it was truly me!

These reactions boosted my confidence immensely. I was thrilled with the changes that were happening in my body. I loved that I was getting stronger and that I could lift more and more each day.

I will never forget the first time I attempted shoulder shrugs. Shoulder shrugs were a huge confidence booster for me because, although I was still small, it seemed like I could lift relatively heavy weight and look strong. I made sure everyone in the gym saw me as I piled on two forty-five-pound plates on each side of the bar. Just as I had planned, I blew through a set of ten reps without any problems.

Then I tried another set.

I made it to about seven reps. I thought it was interesting, so I tried again.

The bar almost slipped out of my hands and fell to the ground before I could finish three reps.

My oversized ego was brought back to reality and I felt small again. Why was I having such a hard time? The weight was not the issue! I could easily lift that bar again, no problem, but something else was keeping me from lifting it consistently.

By this time, I had only been lifting weights for a couple of weeks. As I stared at the bar with frustration, Mike came over to me and showed me his hands. They had calluses all over them. He looked at me and said, "You may be strong enough to lift the weight, but because your hands aren't calloused, you won't be able to lift it for very long."

God spoke so powerfully to me through this illustration and I believe He wants to share it with you as well. Just like the 225-pound bar, the call that God has given you is a weighty thing. You may feel like you could handle it right *now,* but without experience and exposure, your grip will not last as long as you need it to. Sometimes God gives us a glimpse of the call on our lives, and we begin to think that we are ready to carry it TODAY. The reality is that the only way we will be able to carry the call with perseverance is experiencing the callusing process so that our hands can handle the weight. My mom always used to tell me, "Jared, following Jesus is not a sprint, it is a marathon." We must be able to endure to the very end!

From The Pit to The Palace

The pit was just one of the tests God used to form Joseph's call. It created open blisters on his spiritual hands. It cut deep; it was quite painful, but it was absolutely necessary.

You see, without the pit, Joseph would have relied on his circumstances or his surroundings to cause his call to come forth. The pit proved to Joseph that it was God who was truly in control of his purpose, and that He would be the very One who would bring him to his promise. Through this experience, Joseph's hands were beginning to be exposed to the weight of his calling.

God used Reuben as a tool to keep Joseph safe when his brothers had intended to hurt him. No weapon formed against you can prosper when you are in the hands of the God, who causes all things to work together for the good of those who love Him and are called according to His purpose! (See Isaiah 54:17, Romans 8:28)

After being thrown into the pit, Joseph's brothers betrayed him in the worst way possible. They sold him into slavery to a nation that was godless, hostile towards Jehovah's people. But, God was not about to forget about Joseph. No, this was just the beginning.

Now Joseph had been taken down to Egypt. And Potiphar, an officer of Pharaoh, captain of the guard, an Egyptian, bought him from the Ishmaelites who had taken him down there. The Lord was with Joseph, and he was a successful man; and he was in the house of his master the Egyptian. And his master saw that the Lord was with him and that the Lord made all he did to prosper in his hand. So Joseph found favor in his sight, and served him. Then he made him overseer of his house, and all that he had he put under his authority. So it was, from the time that he had made him over-seer of his house and all that he had, that the Lord blessed the Egyptian's house for Joseph's sake; and the blessing of the Lord was on all that he had in the house and in the field. Thus he left all that he had in Joseph's hand, and he did not know what he had except for the bread, which he ate.
Genesis 39:1–6

From the pit to the palace, God had a plan for Joseph, but it was time for a different kind of test. The test of the pit is a difficult and dark one, but is nothing in comparison to the *test of success*. Before we talk about this test, let's talk about the power of promotion.

Just because Joseph had weathered through some trials did not mean that the radical favor on his life was lost in the pit (no pit has the power to destroy your promise). Even without the coat of many colors, Joseph's favor translated all the way over into Egypt and marked him before Potiphar, the Pharaoh's officer, who ended up purchasing Joseph to work for him. He truly went from "the pit to the palace," and before long, he was on his way to the royal chambers.

Let me just say that sometimes favor takes on different forms. In the pasture, favor looked like a robe of many colors. In the palace, it looked like royalty. During the "process," it looked like a pit. Favor led Joseph to all of these places, even the ones he didn't ask for. It's important to understand this because sometimes, favor will lead you into seasons that don't seem favorable, however, just because they aren't favorable at the time doesn't mean that it isn't the friction you need to move you forward. Without friction or resistance, you can't walk effectively.

Do not discount the trials you are going through. It may just be the favor of God at work acting as a 'pit stop' between the pasture and the palace.

Powerful Promotion

Under Potiphar's rule, the text tells us that Joseph was found to be a successful man. The Lord prospered everything he put his hands to. Even in a godless society, Joseph thrived. Potiphar took notice of this and wanted in on the blessing! After witnessing the favor on Joseph's life, Potiphar promoted Joseph to oversee his entire house and all that he owned! God actually uses Joseph's "YES" to prosper his master!

As a young leader, God will bless you and prosper you in many ways, but not simply for your own good. God has an ultimate plan and He is looking to partner with you to carry out His purpose. Here are some ways you can say, "YES" to Godly promotion and blessing:

YOU ARE BLESSED TO BE A BLESSING

God had a plan for Joseph to be in a position of high authority and power far before he could ever imagine it. Yes, Joseph had dreams of his *own,* but considering the circumstances and sequence of events in his journey, it is highly unlikely that he had a full understanding of God's "dream" for him. I am sure he was completely blindsided by the opportunity that was presented to him.

God will bless you and put you in positions of high authority and power for your sake as well as other's. Joseph's favor and prosperity began to bleed into everything he put his hands to. Because of this, Potiphar profited from Joseph's prosperity!

Wherever God has placed you, He has placed you there strategically. Ultimately, it is to further His name and glory, but He wants to use vessels that can declare that it is because of the *favor and blessing of God* that they are prosperous. Through your life, God can influence influential people!

YOUR PURPOSE WILL BRING YOU INFLUENCE

God marked Joseph, out of all the slaves who were up for sale, to be the one who found favor with Potiphar. Slave drivers usually had multiple prospects for their buyers to choose from. What made Joseph so special that Pharaoh's officer chose him? I believe it was because God had marked Joseph with supernatural favor. He may have lost the physical coat of many colors, but favor was not a physical article of clothing, it was divine gift from God to change nations.

The call of God on your life will ultimately bring you before people of power because God's desire is to influence the influential. God has a global vision and wants to use you to shape nations and to transform cities! To do so, God will mark you with something that is only explainable by the anointing of God! Do not be surprised when you find yourself in places that seem to be out of your league! You may not see the physical coat of favor that is upon you, but you have been clothed with a spiritual coat of favor that will bring you to places you could never dream of! Do not disqualify yourself from your destiny!

YOU MAY BE PROMOTED BEFORE YOU EXPECTED

It did not take long for Potiphar to realize that Joseph was special. Everything he touched prospered. After seeing this, Potiphar promoted Joseph over his entire household so he could get in on the blessing.

It is common for young leaders who are obviously called by God to find themselves promoted quite rapidly wherever they go. Whether it is in the pastures of their parent's homeland or the palace of a national leader, you bear the mark of a "called one." Do not be surprised when you are offered positions that seem to be above your pay grade! God will give you supernatural prosperity so that He can accomplish supernatural things through you!

This is something I have experienced, firsthand. One of these experiences was in Redding, California, when I was attending Bethel's School of Supernatural Ministry. I had been frustrated and discouraged because I had walked away from my "dream job" back in Dallas, and felt as if the coat of many colors had been ripped away from me. However, God had prepared a path for me wherever I had gone in the past, to experience promotion and favor, and once again, He had a path prepared for me. As I simply obeyed God and submitted to my "call" to Redding, doors began to open up that I could never have imagined. I was asked to lead worship for the Supernatural School of Ministry and a few months into it, I found myself invited to the Senior Leader's (of Bethel Church) house for a strategic planning meeting for the newly developed Worship Rooms. I had been asked to be a part of the team and walked into the house feeling a bit out of place. I thought to myself, "What made me so special to be invited here?" There were plenty of people who would have loved to be in this position, but for some reason, God chose me!

In the midst of what was going on, I began to doubt my credibility and my right to be there, and argued with the Lord in my heart. As I tried to disqualify myself, I heard the Lord say, "watch this."

As we gathered in the living room, I looked around and saw many high-profile leaders. I felt so privileged to simply be there. The moment a thought came into my head to try and disqualify me, a friend volunteered *ME* to get up and lead worship for everyone. I was a bit shocked, and felt as if God was laughing at me in my spirit.

There I was, a first year student who simply decided to obey God, and was now being given the opportunity to do something I would have never imagined possible. From that point on, I had many doors opened to me, and I am still in shock at how God promoted me in that season.

I could share so many more stories like this about how the favor of God led me to places of influence that I did not deserve or earn. The beauty in all of this is that God can take you from the lowest place of your life and, in an instant, promote you beyond your wildest dreams.

Promotion is never about you being magnified;
it is always about Christ being glorified.

It has nothing to do with showing off how great we are. Promotion "shows off" how amazing and powerful our God is. He can bring you from the pit to the palace in the blink of an eye; He is *that* powerful and *that* good. Walking into situations that are out of your league and prospering in those situations only brings glory to God. Do not shrink back from the promotion that lies ahead of you. Grab it by the horns and direct the praise to the One who got you there!

Have you experienced supernatural promotion? Have you seen the faithfulness of God to your call? Take some time to thank God for the path He has set before you. Ask for humility and integrity to walk the path in truth and righteousness.

Prayer:

God, thank You for all that You have done for me. I am so grateful for all that You have given to me and promised me. Teach me to walk in Your ways and to walk with humility and integrity, even when I am promoted beyond my wildest dreams! I want to glorify You in all that I do.

11

the test of success

J ust a chapter ago, Joseph was in the worst place of his life, and now he's in a palace!

Have you gotten whiplash yet?

Such is the life of an anointed, young leader. The most important thing to remember in all of this is that God is sovereign over the entire process. Every second of every day is under His control and jurisdiction. He is the God of the pit *AND* the God of the palace. The only mistake is to get too attached to one or the other.

So far, Joseph has chosen to honor and serve the Lord. His new position of power has not seduced him into sin or self-serving disobedience, but the test of success is about to manifest right before his eyes. Let's read what happens in the midst of Joseph's great success story:

Now Joseph was handsome in form and appearance.

And it came to pass after these things that his master's wife cast longing eyes on Joseph, and she said, "Lie with me."

But he refused and said to his master's wife, "Look, my master does not know what is with me in the house, and he has committed all that he has to my hand. There is no one greater in this house than I, nor has he kept back anything from me but you, because you are his wife. How then can I do this great wickedness, and sin against God?"

So it was, as she spoke to Joseph day by day, that he did not heed her, to lie with her or to be with her.

But it happened about this time, when Joseph went into the house to do his work, and none of the men of the house was inside, that she caught him by his garment, saying, "Lie with me." But he left his garment in her hand, and fled and ran outside. And so it was, when she saw that he had left his garment in her hand and fled outside, that she called to the men of her house and spoke to them, saying, "See, he has brought in to us a Hebrew to mock us. He came in to me to lie with me, and I cried out with a loud voice. And it happened, when he heard that I lifted my voice and cried out, that he left his garment with me, and fled and went outside."

So she kept his garment with her until his master came home. Then she spoke to him with words like these, saying, "The Hebrew servant whom you brought to us came in to me to mock me; so it happened, as I lifted my voice and cried out, that he left his garment with me and fled outside." So it was, when his master heard the words, which his wife spoke to him, saying, "Your servant did to me after this manner," that his anger was aroused.
Genesis 39:7–19

The test of success is one of the most difficult tests to pass. Yes, it is more difficult than the test of the pit. In the pit, the only one you have to cling to is the Lord. The pit brings you face to face with your Maker. The test of success, however, is quite different.

You see, in seasons of success, everything you have been searching for is easily acquirable. You now live in a palace, and you are second in command. Servants are now serving YOU, and your purpose seems more attainable than ever.

It is much more difficult to search for God when you have everything you could ever need or want. This is when character is truly put to the test. Were you only following Jesus to get to the promise, or the Promise Giver?

Let's walk through some characteristics of the test of success.

SUCCESS IS SEDUCTIVE

Imagine this: you have been called into the palace and have been promoted beyond your wildest dreams. At this point, you have completely forgotten about the pit. You are living in great power and authority and then all of a sudden, BAM: the success that once served you now demands that you serve it.

Joseph has been promoted from the pit to the palace and has truly served his master well. Everything he has done has been incredibly successful, until now. He is faced with a choice: either lean on the words of his (earthly) master or obey the words of his God. Potiphar's wife offers Joseph a shortcut to pleasure and power, but he quickly identifies it as sin, undercover.

Just like Potiphar's wife, sin often disguises itself as the road to success. Only the wise and truly dedicated to God identify this sin as a lie, trying to derail them from their destiny. But, sin is an unrelenting force, and in this case, Potiphar's wife refuses to back down. She begins to entice Joseph and seduce him into bed with her.

Have you ever heard these words before? *"It is no big deal; no one has to know. We deserve this! "*

On the path to your purpose, you will be faced with tempting opportunities that will try to seduce you away from the call of God on your life. They seem harmless and discreet at first; sin always does, but to follow down their path ends in death and destruction. It is a scheme of the devil to rid you of everything God has promised you.

As you can see, this test cannot be taken in the pit. In the seasons of pain and loneliness, we often cling to Jesus because He is all that we have. However, in the season of success, we have options. It is in the moments where we feel powerful and invincible that the enemy comes in with *just* the right opportunity to tempt us.

It is important to realize that the devil is, in fact, very good at his job. He's been doing it for a long time. He is tactful and cunning. He knows exactly how to disguise sin with subtlety to make it seem like it is "no big deal." He convinces the leader that they can handle it. All the while, God sits back, watches, and waits to see if His servant will trust *His* way or the *world's* way.

One of my favorite biblical illustrations of this truth is found in Exodus 33. The people of Israel have completely violated their covenant with God (yet again) and have hurt Him deeply. Because God is not a liar, He refuses to withhold His promises from His people. However, He tells Moses that if He goes with them to the Promised Land, His anger and jealousy would burn so hot that the Israelites would be "consumed." He gives them the option of grabbing hold of their promise, but He will not be a part of it.

Moses' response is incredible. Like a true "friend of God," he replies,

> *"If Your Presence does not go with us,*
> *do not bring us up from here.*
> *Exodus 33:15*

This is the sign of the type of man or woman that God trusts. The promise is never worth anything without God's presence. To walk in this type of favor with God, we must constantly be aware of the enemy's schemes in the seasons of success. God is always the prize. In HIM we have every promise—yes and amen (see 2 Cor. 1:20).

The enemy will throw things in your path that seem easy to overcome. During seasons of success, it can be tempting to dismiss these opportunities as "simple obstacles." Not taking them seriously is one of the most dangerous things you can possibly do. It is when we are relaxed and over-confident that we are most vulnerable to the enemy's attacks. Instead of relying on the strength and conviction of God, we rely on our own success. Second Corinthians 2:11 tells us that we "must not be unaware of the enemy's schemes, lest he outsmart us."

Joseph identifies the enemy's tactics and does not fall for them. He realizes that he has come too far to take any shortcuts. Instead of thinking that he can handle the pressure, he runs out of the palace.

It is of utmost importance for young leaders to know how to discern what success is being offered to them by God and by man. We cannot afford to be young and immature in our decision making— we must live according to the spirit of God to resist the seduction of success and see obedience to God as the only true form of a successful life.

OBEDIENCE IS DANGEROUS

Potiphar's wife does not like Joseph's response to her sexual invitation and decides to retaliate. as Potiphar's slave, Joseph was under the authority of Potiphar's wife. When she commanded him to lay with her, she was seducing him to break the law of his God and the covenant of her marriage. Joseph chose to obey God and disobey his master. Knowing that this could very well be the end of his professional career, he ran from the opportunity to gain success, power, and pleasure through disobedience to God and chose the straight and narrow path.

You will be offered many choices to obey or disobey God to accomplish the call on your life. Whether it is a sexual temptation similar to Joseph's or an unwholesome business transaction, you will be offered various opportunities to do things your own way as opposed to God's way. Some may seem easier than others, but when the right temptation comes knocking at your door (or pulling at your clothes), will you have the resolve to trust in the Lord and say no to sin?

Even good ideas can be bad ideas if they are not "God ideas."

The Biblical definition of sin is to "miss the mark." Sin always offers shortcuts that promise but have no real power to deliver. Only God's way will prosper.

Walking in obedience to God may mean becoming enemies with the world because we are completely "other from" the world. This is revealed to us in 2 Corinthians:

Do not be unequally yoked together with unbelievers. For what fellowship has righteousness with lawlessness? And what communion has light with darkness?
2 Corinthians 6:14

As a young leader, there will be a time when you are faced with rejecting the world's "road to success" and accepting that true success is only found in the Way, the Truth and the Life.

Lastly,

SUCCESS CAN BE DECEPTIVE

If Joseph would have believed his "own press," he might have accepted the woman's invitation. He was handsome and favored, right? Instead of trusting God to get him where he needed to go, he could have relied on connections and earthly wisdom to bring forth his purpose.

Often times when we are successful, we find ourselves forgetting where we came from. We need to be reminded of who actually freed us from the pit and promoted us to the palace, but success works hard to blind God's called to the truth. Pride and arrogance begin to creep in, and we forget that God is still the God of the Pit *and* the Palace.

Guarding your heart from pride and an over-awareness of self will protect you from trusting in YOU instead of the One who is sovereign over all. Remember, your call was a gift.

I have watched this happen with far too many leaders. They have become so aware of their own gifts that they forget that they are, in fact, GIFTS—freely given to them by the Great Giver. If our eyes are on self in the season of success, we will most certainly fall into the trap that the enemy has set before us. Remembering that God is still Lord over the call will empower us to walk in HIS ways and not our own.

Joseph's "YES" opened the door to success, but it is most definitely a test. It is one of the most important tests to pass because it proves your trust in God and His Word. It is easy to trust while in the pit; there is no way of getting out of there without a divine intervention! But the test of success exposes your *true* answer to this question: Can you trust God when you feel like you have everything?

Key Activation:

Are you in a season of success? Have you honored God with your choices? Integrity is honoring God behind closed doors, when no one sees it. Take some time and spend it with the Lord reevaluating this season and recalibrate your heart to be aligned with God's call on your life! If there are places that you have disobeyed, ask God for forgiveness and get back on the path He has set before you.

Prayer:

God, I want to fully trust in You, for better or for worse. Give me the strength to know when an opportunity comes my way that is trying to derail me from my destiny. Lead me not into temptation, but deliver me from evil. Teach me to use my success for Your glory.

12

[sexual purity: leadership with integrity]

I wanted to take an entire chapter to dedicate towards sexual purity, simply because it is one of the most important choices you can make as a young leader in your life, ministry, marriage or future relationship. I have discussed the "spiritual seduction" that leaders face, however I want to address the ACTUAL seduction that we as leaders are faced with every day. The frequency of moral failures, pornography addictions and hidden sexual sin that plague the lives of Christian leaders today is crippling. It seems that another moral failure is exposed and exploited in the media every week. We must take a stand for sexual purity and integrity in our generation of leaders.

As I have already shared in previous chapters, I had a rough past throughout my teenage years. Most of my issues came from a messed up sexual history. My exposure to pornography at such a young age was immensely detrimental to my purity and caused havoc to my life. For twelve straight years I struggled with an addiction to porn and sexuality in relationships. It seemed like a cycle that could never be broken.

When I was eighteen, I was in the middle of choosing where I was going to college when I found out that the pastor of my church had been living in moral failure for a few years. I was completely devastated, but more than I was angry at him for his actions, I was struck with the fear of God concerning my own struggle. I was also doing ministry and struggling with porn—who's to say that I wouldn't end up in the same moral failure as him?

I made a decision that day to deal with my sexuality and attend CFNI where I would be disciple and disciplined in this area. I believe that, because of my choice to attend an out-of-the-ordinary Bible school, God honored my act of faith and delivered me from years of sexual addiction and perversion.

As I write this book, years later, I am able to say that by the grace of God, I live in freedom from sexual immorality. I am also writing this book as a single man—one who knows and understands the fight for sexual purity. There is not a day that I do not have to fight with all of my might to stay pure and resist temptation, but I can tell you that it is the most important fight you will wage.

Our generation is sick and tired of pastors and preachers who are "professional talkers" but never practice what they preach. It is almost impossible for me to walk into a church and not ask myself the question, "I wonder if this pastor is living a life of integrity." This is not a license to be over-critical of pastors and leaders, but it is most certainly a license to be over-critical of yourself and your own integrity.

As young leaders, we must fight to be those who are authentic. Only through authenticity will we truly reach people with a message of freedom. Look at what God's word has to say about leaders who don't walk in liberty:

For speaking out arrogant words of vanity they entice by fleshly desires, by sensuality, those who barely escape from the ones who live in error, promising them freedom while they themselves are slaves of corruption; for by what a man is overcome, by this he is enslaved.
2 Peter 2:18–19

The message against pornography is no longer a message for men only. Recent statistics and polls show more women looking at porn now more than ever before. But sexual purity isn't only about resisting temptation to look at pornography—it is all sexual conduct. This includes singles, engaged and married couples. We must strive to be "above reproach" in our sexuality.

Joseph is described as a "good-looking" young man. The test of seduction was really initiated by a sexual advance that was made upon him by Potiphar's wife, but he had already made a "YES" in his heart for sexual purity. I could write an entire book on the sexual temptations that one will face in ministry or in leadership, however, before we get into the ways you can say, "YES" to purity, it is important to understand these few points about leadership:

POWER IS ATTRACTIVE

As a leader, people will naturally be drawn to you. Whether it is because of your charisma, good looks, charm, talent, gifting, or simply your position, you will find yourself surrounded by people who want to get in on the power you possess. It is important to realize that this is a normal part of the human existence, we all want to be a part of something significant. However, it can lead us into some serious problems if we follow the lust for power. Be aware that your position as a leader will draw all types of people, some who are after you for what you carry!

Knowing this is not to make you jaded or cynical of the people who desire your time, it is to call attention to the importance of walking in wisdom and awareness of your surroundings. A lot of people will want your time, but setting boundaries for yourself may protect you from being overrun by the masses of followers that are pulling at you!

DISCRETION IS WISE

It is critically important to know how to handle the position that God has given you. To be able to do this, you must have discretion and discernment. As a leader, you are the *initiator* and the people following you are the *responders*. You may not be able to control the way that someone feels about you, but you can control the way that you handle yourself around him or her. Always be wise to surround yourself with accountability and covering. Never allow yourself to be alone in a room with someone of the opposite sex. Live a transparent life before your leaders and inform them of everything that is going on behind closed doors. If something happens that is questionable, confess it to your leadership immediately and get covered.

About a year ago, a pastor from another church approached me because he had seen a picture of me preaching at Youth Church on a social network. It was summer time and I had worn a tank top without thinking. I live in Texas so the heat is sometimes unbearable. In Abilene, there is a bit of a "laid back" vibe, so it did not occur to me that I was doing anything wrong.

He told me that as a good-looking young man with a muscular build, I should be more careful with how I carried myself. In my head, I had no sinful desire or impure motive, but hearing this pastor's perspective made me so upset that I wept after getting off the phone with him. I never wanted to mislead anyone, so I quickly took the picture down and became more aware of what I wore in front of my students. It seems silly, but I believe it is moments like these that determine the caliber of leader you are.

You must also be wise with your power. Do not abuse it to manipulate or seduce people to yourself. This will only come back to bite you, and you will find yourself in a world of mess. As Christian leaders, we are called to direct the "Bride of Christ" to Jesus. If we turn her eyes onto ourselves, we are no longer a friend of the Bridegroom, but a competitor.

SELF-CONTROL IS NECESSARY

Whether you are single or married, you are probably like the majority of the population and have a sex drive. This is not wrong, and it definitely is not evil, however, it is something that must be tamed and submitted under the control of the Holy Spirit.

As leaders, we all have good days and bad days. As I discussed earlier in the chapter, sometimes our most vulnerable moments come when we think that we are strong enough to handle any temptation that comes our way. However, sometimes it is the exact opposite.

I have personally found the most vulnerable place of temptation to be right after a huge victory. A great illustration of this is the story of Elijah and Mt. Carmel. Elijah had just defeated the prophets of Baal and the prophetesses of Ashtoreth by calling down fire from heaven. After the showdown was over, he finds out that Jezebel is looking for him and wants to kill him. He runs for his life and has a meltdown. Even after an incredible display of God's faithfulness and power, Elijah slips into depression and spiritual vulnerability:

> *But he himself went a day's journey into the wilderness, and came and sat down under a broom tree. And he prayed that he might die, and said, "It is enough! Now, Lord, take my life, for I am no better than my fathers!"*
> *1 Kings 19:4*

It is in these times that the enemy comes in to seduce us with temptations that can offer us another rush or hit of excitement. Just like in the test of success, when we are in the low points of our journey, the enemy convinces us that to continue fighting is a lost cause and that we might as well give in to temptation that can alleviate our temporary frustration. Whether it be flirting with someone who is not your spouse or watching porn on your smart phone, sin always promises to make us feel better; to give us what we are currently lacking. Remember this: sin is always a lie. It promises, but it never delivers.

The bottom line is that, sadly, there are too many leaders falling into sexual sin and putting their congregations in jeopardy. We have a responsibility to the people that we are leading to live lives of integrity, character, and honesty. That means submitting our bodies to the power of the Holy Spirit . Paul says it this way:

> *But I discipline my body and bring it into subjection, lest, when I have preached to others, I myself should become disqualified.*
> *1 Corinthians 9:27*

We cannot lead others if we cannot first lead ourselves. We cannot lead ourselves unless the Holy Spirit first leads us.

Here are a few ways you can say, "YES" to a life of purity and leadership with integrity.

CHANGE YOUR PERSPECTIVE

MEN: Our society has taught us that it's culturally acceptable to, when a girl passes by, look at her boobs and butt to see "what she's got." We've trained ourselves to inspect her sexually before we interact with her spiritually. This is wrong for a couple of reasons. First of all, the girl might be beautiful on the outside but dead and disgusting on the inside. Looks can be deceiving, and I know she might have that thigh-gap but she also might have a spiritual-gap that will last for eternity. The other one will probably go away when she has kids.

MEN & WOMEN: Secondly, we end up training our perspective to first look for physical or sexual attributes that attract us instead of seeing them for who they really are. Perceiving someone of the opposite sex this way keeps us in a sexually charged state. Look, I'm not saying that you shouldn't be attracted to your mate, but I am saying that Biblical attraction goes deeper than how she looks in yoga pants or how great his hair is. The Bible tells us to,

"Know no one after the flesh." (2 Cor. 5:16)

This means that we should be looking to connect with people's spirits, not just their sexuality. Once we change our perspective, we begin to interact with people in a way that truly discovers who they are.

MAKE AN EYE COVENANT

This comes from the book of Job:

"I made a covenant with my eyes, not to look lustfully at a woman." (Job 31:1)

MEN & WOMEN: The eyes are more than just lenses to behold beauty; they are gateways to our soul. This means that whatever we let ourselves behold, we will ultimately become. I used to think that this was a silly idea, until I put it into practice. There's something about a "covenant" that releases to us a powerful grace to keep it. If you study what a covenant actually was in the Old Testament, you'd realize that it is not something that can simply be broken by divorce papers—or even an unfaithful act. A covenant is something binding by blood, water and spirit. When we make a covenant with our eyes we decide to alter our lifestyle based upon the severity of the covenant we have made. This allows us to take it seriously and guard ourselves from anything that would try to divide it.

By guarding our eyes, we refuse to look at someone of the opposite sex in a way that would objectify them for our own sexual gratification. We refuse to look at porn as a way to appease our momentary desire. We must control our eye gates before anything else; they lead to our very souls!

DON'T COUNT YOURSELF OUT

MEN & WOMEN: There are two common mistakes that Christian leaders make when dealing with sexual sin. The first is to soften its sting by making amends for it out of compassion for the one struggling. I understand this approach, simply because I have been pastoring young people for years who consistently share with me about their struggles. However, coddling someone's sin is not a way to deal with it—it simply makes it worse.

The other mistake Christian leaders make is to communicate the idea that, because we have the power of the Holy Spirit, one should never struggle or deal with sexual sin again. By doing this, they create unrealistic expectations for the believer. When they mess up, they feel disqualified and shamed.

The only way to deal with sexual sin is to deal with it realistically—and that means Biblically. Do we have the power of the Holy Spirit in us to keep us from sinning? ABSOLUTELY. Are we going to sin again? PROBABLY. You're not counted out because you messed up, but just because you messed up and God has grace for you DOESN'T mean it's not a big deal. Let's strive to kill this stuff while having grace for ourselves and others—and let's not do it alone.

TRUST GOD'S TIMING

SINGLES & ENGAGED COUPLES: I truly believe that the main reason for sexual failure is due to a lack of trust in God's timing. Let me lay it out for you like this:

"A wife does not have authority over her own body but yields it to her husband. In the same way, a husband does not have authority over his own body but yields it to his wife." (1 Cor. 7:4)

The Bible is basically telling us here that the power of our orgasm belongs to our spouse. It might seem explicit, but if we're really getting down to what the text is trying to say, that's what it's telling us. Now, I know what you're thinking—"What if I don't have a spouse?" Good question. Who does your body belong to?

"An unmarried girl (or guy) or virgin is can be fully devoted to the Lord and can focus on being holy in her (or his) BODY and spirit." (1 Cor. 7:34)

As a single, young leader, our bodies belong to the Lord. I know that completely goes against culture's message of taking control of our own sexuality, but it's the truth. When we choose to masturbate or look at porn as a sexual release we take control of our sexuality instead of trusting in God's timing. Yes, we were created with a sex drive and sexual desires. These aren't sinful or wrong—but activating them outside of God's design IS. When we take our sexuality into our own hands (pun intended) we choose to take control of our lives instead of giving control to the Lord. In our season of singleness, we are called to trust God and His timing concerning our sexuality.

I know this can be difficult and sometimes, seem impossible. Every time I write on this, someone comments or messages me telling me how it is healthy for people to masturbate and how my stance on it is outdated or limiting. I believe they are just plain wrong. Masturbation, even without lust being the driving factor, will lead to lust. It will awaken sexuality before its time. Sexual desire has a way of snowballing—it wants more, the more you feed it. So although, it may be possible to masturbate without lusting, I guarantee that the more you do it, the more you will desire it. The more you desire it, the harder it will be to keep from lusting. Plus, sex was intended for two people—not one.

BE TRANSPARENT

SINGLES & ENGAGED COUPLES: Sexual purity is not about never making a mistake. It's not perfection. In fact, no one is perfect and chances are you will slip up. The key to sexual purity is transparency. What does this mean? It means that you refuse to let anything stay hidden in your life. Sin only has power in the dark.

Whenever I find myself being tempted or falling short, I call my mentor. I let him know what happened and how it happened. Can I be honest with you? I hate those calls. It has never gotten easier after all these years—but I do it because I know that as long as my sin stays hidden, it has power over me—shame, guilt and another opportunity to just give up and keep sinning. The power is not in being able to say "I've never sinned." You won't connect with anyone that way. The power is in being able to say, "there are people in my life that know everything I struggle with and keep me accountable to my purpose."

Get a mentor—someone who you're a bit afraid of telling your "stuff" to. Let them in on what's going on in your life and don't hold back. There's freedom and healing in sharing your struggle with someone else. You can't do this alone and you weren't meant to!

DO WHATEVER YOU'VE GOT TO DO

"If your right hand causes you to sin, cut it off. It's better to be without a hand than for your whole body to burn in hell." (Matt. 5:30)

Just like Joseph, we need to do whatever is necessary to run from temptation. We've got to know our triggers and deal with them. Do you find yourself tempted to masturbate or look at porn more when you have long periods of idle time ahead? Is it your phone late at night? Twitter? Instagram? Is it when you and your girlfriend are Netflix & Chilling?

Look—whatever it is, deal with it. Don't let anything have power over you.

***Sometimes we have to sacrifice CONVENIENCE
for the sake of our CONVICTIONS.***

Do whatever you have to do to keep yourself from falling into temptation so that you can guard your sexuality from guilt and shame.

YOUNG LEADERS: Integrity is defined as who we are when no one is watching. It is time to get serious about sexual purity and break the enemy's stronghold in our lives! If you are struggling with sexual sin, it is time to expose it. Go to someone that you can trust and get it out in the open. Tell your leader or your pastor. Deal with it now so it will not deal with you later. Choose today to live a life of integrity so that when success tries to seduce you back into slavery, you emerge victorious!

Activation:

Are you living in a life of integrity? Have you been struggling and keeping it a secret? Have you stopped fighting to live in sexual purity? Talk to a leader today about what's going on in your life. Don't let your sin stay hidden any longer. It's time to move it out of the dark and into the light. Repent and make a decision to be a leader that lives with integrity.

Prayer:

God, I want to live a lifestyle of purity that pleases you and reaches others. I repent of my sin and I turn from my wicked ways. I make a covenant before you with my eyes to never look with lust towards someone again. Give me the strength and courage to be the leader you created me to be!

13

the curse of being misunderstood

Then Joseph's master took him and put him into the prison, a place where the king's prisoners were confined. And he was there in the prison.
Genesis 39:20

My Worst Nightmare

My first year as a youth pastor was one of the most bizarre and difficult years of my life. There were so many crazy things that happened that year and I am determined to one day write a book documenting as many as I can remember, this is one story I will never forget.

When I first came to the church where I currently serve, the youth ministry was struggling. A transition of leadership had just occurred and the number of students was few. It seemed as if no one knew what to do or where to go. I had just come out of Bible school and I was ready to see revival take over a city, but it did not seem like this was the place where I would see that happen!

The Lord put it on my heart to spend the first couple of months taking the students that stayed in the ministry (after I had made the transition as Youth Pastor) through my discipleship curriculum. This process of discipleship would help the transition so that who remained could become my student leaders and create a new culture in our youth ministry that would be conducive for a move of God.

I had twelve students to my home—six guys and six girls. I was very intentional about the way I interacted with the students, especially the girls. As a young, single pastor, I had to make sure the boundaries were set to create a healthy environment for them, and a safe environment for me. I made sure that every time they were at my house the guys were present, and another leader as well. I did everything in my power to act with integrity, and I can honestly say that my motives were always pure before God. However, my actions were misconstrued and misunderstood. Some of the parents had never seen a youth pastor take such initiative with their children and began to question why I would care so much. A parent of one of my students started spreading rumors about me. They referred to me as a "molester" to other parents, and slandered my reputation, which caused some of my students to leave the group. My reputation—along with my heart—was deeply wounded.

Nothing could have been further from the truth. I could not grasp how I could be so misunderstood when I so desired to honor God by investing in these young people. I also could not understand how God could allow this to happen. Because this was one of my first real issues as a new pastor, it was devastating to me. Even though my pastoral leadership covered me and supported me, I was incredibly hurt. For fear of being further misunderstood, I isolated myself, and for a few months, completely withdrew from my students.

When you are called to have influence, you are constantly in the limelight. Because your life is on display for all to see, there will be times that you will be falsely accused and persecuted for doing what God has called you to do. It seems to happen when you feel like you are in the center of God's will, living out your calling in obedience. All of a sudden, you get blind-sided by a situation that just knocks you off your feet. This is what happened to me, and this is what happened to Joseph.

Joseph was doing everything God had called him to do and in one instant, everything he had worked for was taken from him. Not only was it stripped from his hands but now, due to a false accusation, his reputation was completely ruined.

In my own life, this has always been my biggest fear: the fear of being misunderstood. *I* know that my heart is pure and my intentions are from a place of integrity, but what happens when the people I am leading do not see that?

There have been so many times in my life where I have been misunderstood. Including the above story, ministry has been rife with name-calling, rumors, slander of all kinds, including in public settings, social networks, and even the destruction of my personal property.

People who have stepped up to make a difference for God must expect to be stepped on by those who don't understand.

This cannot be overlooked in the story of Joseph. He had worked so hard to honor God with his choices and now, not only were they not being seen, they were being misconstrued as something that was false.

Because your influence will bring you before many opinions, you will ALWAYS struggle with the fear of being misunderstood. The reason you have this fear is not negative; it is actually a positive aspect of your heart! Your desire is for people to know Christ and to lead them in the ways of righteousness, so when that comes across the wrong way, it hurts you deeply, because that was never your intention.

This actually happened just a few days ago. I had written a section in this book and shared a personal story between a friend and I that I had not asked for permission to share. After reading it, my friend called me, hurt and frustrated. He shared with me how he felt that I had betrayed his trust and slandered him in public writing. When he told me how he had felt, all I could do was cry. My intentions were never to hurt him; I only had a desire to help people through a situation that he and I had grown through. But because I am human, I made a huge mistake and upset him deeply. I never intended for my actions to be taken as they were, but oftentimes we are misunderstood, as people see things differently than we do.

Let me save you a lot of grief: if Jesus, the Son of God, was one of the most misunderstood people on the planet, God will most certainly allow you to walk through the frustration of being misunderstood.

So what do you do when people believe the worst about you? How do you deal with the internal struggle of being misunderstood?

Here are some ways you can say, "YES" to God in the seasons of being misunderstood.

Working Through Misunderstanding

ASK GOD TO SEARCH YOUR HEART

Whenever there is a misunderstanding, false accusation, or case made against you, it is imperative that you take the time to allow the Holy Spirit to search your heart. One of the most important things I have learned over the years is to pray the prayer that the Psalmist David prayed,

> *Search my heart, Oh God, and know me! Test me and know my thoughts. See if there be anything grievous in me and lead me in the way of everlasting life!*
> *Psalm 139:23–24*

This prayer has become engrained in my mind because I know that there are times that I move too quickly. Instead of dealing with the issues that could arise, I end up having to deal with them AFTER they have already happened.

This is exactly what happened in the story with my friend who was upset about my writing. I moved too quickly and did not think about the outcome of my actions. Taking the time to allow the Lord to shine the light of His love upon us will soften our hearts to be able to receive any correction He might want to show us. This softness of heart will allow you to right your wrongs and lead from humility.

REPENT OF ANY WRONG MOTIVE

If the Lord has spoken anything to you after you have asked Him to search your heart, it is so important to repent of those wrong motives and change the way we think and act. Repentance, in its original meaning, means to change the way you think. You cannot change your actions until your mind has been renewed.

> *"Do not conform to the likeness of this world, but be trans-*
> *formed by the renewing of your mind."*
> *Romans 12:2*

Almost every time I have been falsely accused or misunderstood, I have been convicted of something that I could have done better. Even when the person on the other end is completely in the wrong, there is always something I can learn from the situation and apply to my own personal growth.

Even though the situation with the parent who slandered my reputation was out of left field, I realized I could have connected better with the parents before I connected with their children. This would have given them the opportunity to get to know me better. With that trust established, we could have avoided the situation all together.

The Lord may show you how your attitude or response was inappropriate or unwise. Repentance is a gift from God that can change the way we think and align our mindset with Christ. Repent and move on.

ALLOW GOD TO FIGHT YOUR BATTLES

It is such a temptation for leaders to try to defend themselves against those who are falsely accusing them. I have watched it time after time, whether it is on social media, through a text message, or even in a sermon. Leaders who try to defend themselves always end up making things worse. Look at what God promises:

> *"The Lord is your mighty defender, perfect and just in all his*
> *ways; Your God is faithful and true; he does what is right and fair."*
> *Deuteronomy 32:4*

God assures us that He will be our sword and our shield. He simply asks that we allow Him to fight our battles, on our behalf. To a strong and driven personality, this can seem like inaction, but to God, it is faith and surrender to His goodness and His love for us. It will be your greatest temptation to fight for yourself, but in the end,

139

you cannot win the battles that belong to the Lord. Trust in God and allow Him to be your Defender.

As Joseph sat at the bottom of the prison, you can believe that the sting of being misunderstood was unbearable, but never in the story do we see Joseph arguing his case. He trusted in the Lord, even in the midst of trials, to also be the God over the Prison and to get him to his purpose.

Being misunderstood is a part of the call. You cannot make public impact without public scrutiny and criticism. I have found that the ones who are willing to criticize are usually the ones who aren't doing anything to help or make a difference.

Critics are usually those with loud voices and little accomplishments.

Encourage yourself in the Lord by remembering that even Jesus was misunderstood and truly empathizes with you in your frustration. You are not alone and knowing that God is for you will make all the difference!

<u>*Activation:*</u>

Have you experienced the curse of being misunderstood? Has the experience created in you the fear of man? How has the fear of being misunderstood changed the way you obey the voice of the Lord? Take some time to submit this to the Lord and ask for freedom to fully live out the call on your life!

<u>*Prayer:*</u>

God, I realize that there has been a fear of man in my heart out of fear of being misunderstood. I have been more concerned with my reputation than my obedience to You. Forgive me and release my heart into freedom to fully obey Your call and live in the exhilaration of Your Spirit!

14

the prison

Then Joseph's master took him and put him into the prison, a place where the king's prisoners were confined. And he was there in the prison.
Genesis 39:20

That is right. First came the pit; now the prison. Joseph's journey was far from over. I can hear you saying, "Not again. I thought we dealt with this already, God? Did not he pass this test?"

I thought the same thing, too. It is funny; I have received many prophetic words that have told me that I possess a "life like Joseph." From where I stand, it can feel very discouraging! How much more does this guy have to go through?

The Staircase of Life

Many times, it seems like we are faced with the same trials repeatedly. Have you ever felt like you were going through the same test you just came out of? It can be one of life's most frustrating experiences when you feel as if you are moving backwards.

My mother gave me one of the most powerful illustrations concerning walking through similar trials. She sat me down during a difficult trial that I felt I had overcome victoriously, and learned the lesson God wanted to teach me.

She shared with me a vision that the Lord had given her as a young person:

"Jared, life is like a staircase. You go up three steps and reach a landing. You then go up three more steps and reach another landing. If you are not paying attention, it can seem like you are at the same place you were three steps ago. But, there is a big difference: although it may look and feel exactly the same, you are three steps higher."

Growth consists of learning lessons over and over again in different seasons, places and positions of life.

Joseph had learned the lesson in the *pit* when he had left the *pasture,* but he had never learned this lesson of the *prison* when he left the *palace.*

Both the pit and the prison were places where Joseph was required to trust in God's ability to get him to his purpose without the help of any man or woman, situation or circumstance. God had to do it supernaturally, and He had done it years before, but would He do it again?

Joseph was learning the same lesson, just three steps higher, however, there is a distinction between the pit and the prison:

The Pit was a consequence of Joseph's "YES" to his call.
The Prison was a consequence of Joseph's "YES" to character.

It was not enough for him to trust God to get him from the pit to the palace. He needed to know that God could get him from prison of false accusation all the way back to his promise of his purpose.

The Four Emotions of the Prison

God wants to teach you that there is no natural way for you to accomplish the calling on your life outside of His divine intervention. *He* has to be the one to do it, and God will go to great lengths to show you His ability in the midst of impossible circumstances.

That is why the pit and the prison are absolute necessities. I hope you are beginning to see this truth. However, the prison is described in much greater detail and much greater pain than the first one.

In the pit, we talked about the loneliness and betrayal that we walk through in our journey. In the prison, Joseph experiences *four very intense emotions* that you will also face throughout your life and call. These are also keys that act as guides to understanding the season of the pit.

CAST OUT

Joseph had made a name for himself in Egypt as a successful and prosperous man. Now, due to this false accusation by Potiphar's wife, he became known as a sexual deviant and a homewrecker. Although the claims against him were completely untrue, Joseph had to deal with the shame and embarrassment of being an outcast in society. He was escorted from the palace to the prison and was thrown away, like the rest of the decay of Egyptian society.

This was no place for a man of God.

Can you imagine what was going through Joseph's head right now?

"God how does this work? I have already been betrayed and sold into slavery from my brothers, now you send me to prison? This is worse than the pit! What did I do wrong? I obeyed you! I did not even sleep with the woman and I still have the sentence of an adulterer. I do not understand."

There are times in our lives where injustices befall us as the people of God. While living a life of obedience, we can find ourselves up against the sinful, perverse system of this world that often times works against us.

It is in these times when you are cast out that God becomes your vindication. It may seem that, in the moment, all anyone can see, including yourself, is a mess, but God promises never to let those who trust in Him be put to shame (see Psalm 25:3).

Have you ever heard of how gold is refined? I remember watching a video on the process of gold purification that spoke deeply to me. After harvesting it from the rock, they beat the gold down into fine particles that they then transfer to a chemically treated liquid, which separates the gold from any impurities. The gold sinks to the bottom and the impurities rise to the top. When you look into the basin, all which is visible to the untrained eye is the "dross," which just looks like muck and mire, but beneath that mess is the precious gold, waiting to be revealed as one of the most valuable and beautiful elements known to man.

When the world (or even the church) labels you an outcast, God labels you adopted. When all you can see is the muck and the mire, know that God is refining you as a leader, powerful and pure. He is getting ready to reveal your beauty to the world around you and has kept you close to His heart throughout the entire process.

FORGOTTEN

In chapter 40, Joseph interprets dreams for a baker and a butler. You can refer to the story and read this on your own, but I will summarize it for you here.

The baker has a dream that is interpreted to be about his death, while the butler has a dream that is interpreted to be about the reinstatement of his job. Joseph tells them both that they will be called before the Pharaoh and given a sentence, one for life, and the other for death. He urges them to remember him when they stand before Pharaoh and to tell Pharaoh of the man who interpreted their dreams. Unfortunately, neither of them remembers Joseph, and he stays locked away in the prison for two years.

Have you ever felt like everyone else around you is moving into promotion or progression, while you are the only one that is staying stationary? I was speaking to a friend of mine the other day. As she nears her Bible school graduation, she was still unsure of her plans, and was sharing her frustration with me by phone. She shared with me how she felt like everyone around her was being promoted and progressing to the next place in his or her life, and she was simply stuck where she was.

There are many times in which the Lord puts us into a holding pattern, a place of waiting in which to teach us patience, but these seasons seem as if they will never end. In fact, sometimes, we feel utterly forgotten. It seems as if God has left us to rot in the prison while everyone else moves on. Our mind reminisces of who we were and what we had before we lost it all, and before we know it, we have spiraled into depression and frustration with our current state.

There will be many times in the course of your call when you feel like nothing is happening. You may feel forgotten and ultimately, given up on. These are the moments when we learn patience and trust in God's timing and His faithfulness to cause all things to work together for our good. When you feel forgotten, God invites you to trust in His faithfulness.

USED

Not only was Joseph forgotten, he was used for the sake of his gifts. He got the baker and the butler out of prison and was left there with no promotion or way out for himself!

Having grown up in the church, I was often used for my musical gifting. Sometimes it felt like I was just an instrument to be used whenever it was needed. The feeling of being taken advantage of for what you can produce is one of the most frustrating things that leaders may deal with.

In reality, you may be incredibly gifted and/or talented. Many people will want to use you for those gifts and talents without prioritizing you as a *person*. You may find yourself feeling like Joseph at the bottom of the prison; alone and abandoned by everyone who has used you to get where they want to be. You may ask God, "What's in it for me? When do I get to be the beneficiary of my own gifting?"

If you are interested in leading people to Jesus, you must be prepared to be the bridge between people and their purpose. That means that you will be walked on and used. People will take advantage of you and forget about you even when you have done so much to help them. The only way to avoid bitterness and anger is to realize that everything you do, you do unto the Lord.

If your service is done for the sake of people's affirmation or reimbursement (whether it be spiritual or tangible), you will constantly feel let down by others. However, if everything you do is done for the person of Jesus, you cannot be taken advantage of. What you do is a gift unto the Lord. In the moments that you feel used, remember that God is utilizing you to advance His purposes. God is not only interested in USING you. Before God ever used you, He loved you.

DEPRESSED

Have you ever asked yourself, "Is this what my life is going to be like forever?" Maybe you are working a 9 to 5 and know you have a call to full time ministry. Maybe you are in a season of waiting and it feels like there is no light at the end of the tunnel. Maybe you are just sick and tired of your leadership position, and cannot wait for the day that it all is over. Whatever it may be, you are facing the feelings of despair.

Do not think for a second that Joseph, in the course of two years in prison, did not think to himself, *"Am I ever going to get out of here?"*

No matter how spiritual you are, you will face a time when you ask this question. The very prophet of God, John the Baptist asked a similar question when he was in prison facing a death sentence. He had been waiting years for the coming of the Messiah and everything around him made it seem like he had missed it. He cried out, *"Is this really it? Is Jesus really the messiah or did I get it wrong (Matthew 11:1–19)?"*

In the midst of despair, it is common to begin to question our call and our purpose. Did we miss it? Did we make a mistake? What could we have done differently that could have enabled us to avoid this mess we are in?

We play through the movie of our lives in our heads and spiral deeper and deeper into the frustrations of despair. *"This is it. It is not going to change; there's no way out"*

Joseph went from a place of favor and success to a place of frustration and sadness. Like him, you will find yourself in seasons like this. If you have not walked through it yet, I promise you that at some point, you will. The prison invokes despair because it makes you feel as if there is no way out. All you see is darkness. It is a prison with no windows or doors, and you begin to believe that this will be your life forever. At least the pit had an open ceiling! You can begin to think that the dreams God promised you were lies, and that the calling was a sham.

It is in these moments that God calls you out of depression and into dependency. The enemy wants to convince you that everything God said to you was a lie, and that nothing He promised will come to pass. But, God is calling leaders to such a level of faith and dependence on Him that they can laugh in the face of the enemy.

Knowing the truth will empower you to laugh at the enemy's lies and see God in the midst of the dungeon. This is where your breakthrough happens: faith in the midst of frustration. Even when the prison has no light, the Light of the World lives in you and will shine His goodness upon you once more.

This is your ticket out of the pit; complete and total dependence on God with an unwavering faith in His Word!

Seasons of Hiddenness

We have spoken in previous chapters about how God will often promote you before you expected it. But what happens when you know you're called to promotion but God hasn't seemed to get around to it yet?

There will be seasons in our lives as young leaders where God puts us in "holding patterns." Have you ever seen a plane that in such a position? Their destination is the airport but because of traffic or weather, they are put into a "holding pattern." This usually means flying around in a circular motion until landing can take place.

Often times, when we find ourselves in the prison of life, we can get discouraged because, like the plane, we know our destination. We are convinced of where we are supposed to go, yet it seems like God has forcefully sat us in time out. This is a season of "hiddenness" and before we go any further, I must warn you about trying to escape from this place out of turn.

I have many friends who have counseled me on how to promote myself or move my platform forward. Through manipulating social media or networking relationships with people that have power, it is quite common to see such practices done amongst young leaders to "expose" themselves to the world. Let me be quite clear:

God-given promotion is God-sustained promotion. Man-manipulated promotion must be sustained by man and will ultimately, fail.

Let me encourage you if you are currently in a season of hidden-ness: God knows where to find you when He wants to promote you. You are not responsible for promoting yourself or moving yourself forward. All you are responsible for is being obedient to God's voice and submissive to His timing.

Joseph longed to find breakthrough in his relationships with the baker and the butler but soon learned that only God can promote. All he was responsible to do was to be who God called him to be in every season—he just needed to say, "YES."

Don't be too eager to leave the prison before it's time. Let God be the one to promote you when He sees fit.

Favor in Prison

There is one last thing that I would like to point out to you about the prison, and I believe it is critically important. I could probably write a completely separate book on this one idea, but I will refrain and write a simple paragraph on the matter. The text says something that is very interesting about Joseph before the baker and the butler forget about him:

> *But the Lord was with Joseph and showed him mercy, and He gave him favor in the sight of the keeper of the prison. And the keeper of the prison committed to Joseph's hand all the prisoners who were in the prison; whatever they did there, it was his doing. The keeper of the prison did not look into anything that was under Joseph's authority, because the Lord was with him; and whatever he did, the Lord made it prosper.*
> *Genesis 39:21–23*

Even in the prison, God's favor never left Joseph. Even in the worst of circumstances, God allowed Joseph to thrive in his surroundings.

DON'T FORGET TO LOOK FOR FAVOR
WHEN YOU'RE FRUSTRATED

Here is my last challenge to you:

Are you ignoring or rejecting God's favor because you are in a situation that is not comfortable or enjoyable? Has your attitude been stuck in one or more of the four emotions with which Joseph struggled? Often times we miss the opportunities in the prison because we are so preoccupied with our own frustration.

God will make a table for you in the presence of your enemies. You just have to be willing to sit down and eat, even if it is not what you wanted for dinner.

Activation:

Do you feel like you are in a prison? Take some time to write down the things you are feeling in this season and ask God to show you what He is trying to teach you in the midst of the prison.

Prayer:

God, give me grace to persevere in this season. Give me strength to keep my heart from moving into despair and protect my faith in what You have promised me! I commit my heart to trusting in You!

15

propelled with power

After two years of sitting in prison, Joseph finally gets a break. Pharaoh has a disturbing dream, and after exhausting all of his mystics, he finds that he still has no interpretation. His butler, however, remembers a man in the prison who accurately interpreted his dream and recommends Joseph to do the job. He is brought before Pharaoh and listens closely to his mysterious visions.

Joseph goes on to interpret the dream as a prophetic word from God. The dream (found in Exodus 41) spoke of two seven-year seasons. One season would be seven years of plenty, the other, seven years of famine. Not only did Joseph end up interpreting the dream accurately, he gave wise counsel to Pharaoh on how to prepare for the seven-year famine by taking advantage of the years of plenty.

Because of Joseph's insight and instruction, Pharaoh reinstates him in the kingdom, except this time, Joseph would not be second in command. Pharaoh put Joseph in charge of *his* entire household. If that was not enough, he takes off his royal ring and puts it on Joseph's finger, giving him charge over ALL of Egypt. Let's read what Pharaoh has to say to Joseph:

> *So the advice was good in the eyes of Pharaoh and in the eyes of all his servants. And Pharaoh said to his servants, "Can we find such a one as this, a man in whom is the Spirit of God?"*

> *Then Pharaoh said to Joseph, "Inasmuch as God has shown you all this, there is no one as discerning and wise as you. You*

shall be over my house, and all my people shall be ruled according to your word; only in regard to the throne will I be greater than you." And Pharaoh said to Joseph, "See, I have set you over all the land of Egypt."

Then Pharaoh took his signet ring off his hand and put it on Joseph's hand; and he clothed him in garments of fine linen and put a gold chain around his neck. And he had him ride in the second chariot, which he had; and they cried out before him, "Bow the knee!" So he set him over all the land of Egypt. Pharaoh also said to Joseph, "I am Pharaoh, and without your consent no man may lift his hand or foot in all the land of Egypt."
Genesis 41:37–44

Before I go on to talk about Joseph's incredible promotion, I would like to point out an interesting fact in the story.

If you look at the text, you will realize that Joseph was *not* the one to whom God spoke. Of course, God *used* Joseph to interpret what He was saying to Pharaoh, but I find it intriguing that God spoke directly to Pharaoh first.

You Are Needed

The other day I received a letter in the mail that looked like legal jargon. I never receive anything in the mail other than bills and trash, so I figured it was junk mail. My friend Tim was in town and noticed that I had crumpled it up, and was about to throw it in the trash. He asked me to see the paper and I threw it over to him, laughing at the fact that he would want to see it.

Tim has an incredible business mind. He reads the fine print and can make sense of the "legal jargon" that I simply do not understand. As he read through the papers, he began to explain to me that it was a lawsuit, and the company was reaching out to me as one of their customers who was possibly entitled to compensation. My jaw dropped! Could I receive money from this? I unwrinkled the papers and filled them out, all the while thinking of how foolish I felt without Tim's help!

People who do not know God are like people who do not understand legal jargon. It is addressed to them, but because they do not have an understanding for what it could mean, they often times disregard the message as "junk mail." Without an interpreter who knows how to discover the secrets of the information, they could miss out on an incredible opportunity to receive something incredibly valuable!

People who know God and know His voice are like Tim. They understand the message's meaning, and they relay it accurately. However, the message was not given to them to deliver to the recipient; it was sent directly to the person of intent. Without an interpreter, the recipient is lost, but because of someone who knows how to read and understand the message, the recipient can benefit greatly from it.

God will put you in places of influence to interpret His voice for the world!

It is important to realize that God speaks even to those who do not have a relationship with Him, especially people in positions of influence. He wants to reveal things to them, but often times uses an interpreter who knows His voice to make sense of the message. YOU are that interpreter, and God will call you in moments of great need to aid those in power. Be ready, because influential people NEED your gift!

"Only God Could Do That"

Have you noticed the whiplash is back? The guy who was just in prison for two years gets called out to translate the meaning of a dream filled with cows and plants, and then gets promoted over all of Egypt.

It seems crazy, does not it? Joseph's entire story feels like the wildest rollercoaster ride imaginable. One moment he is in the lowest place of his life, but before you know it, he's higher than ever before.

You see, Joseph's life was supposed to be crazy. That was the point. And often times, your life will be the same way. You could be at your "lowest low" but then, in the course of a couple of minutes, be promoted to the highest high you have ever experienced. Why is it that we experience these drastic changes in position?

I believe God wants to use people who are able to say, "Only God could have done that." He desires stories and testimonies so crazy that, when people look at the lives of these leaders, there is no question that they could not have achieved their position or status without God's intervention. It is through these lives that God is radically glorified. He will not share His glory with anyone and He alone can be responsible for his or her success!

Knowing this truth can strengthen our trust in God in the midst of seasons that seem to make no sense. Truly believing Romans 8:31, which tells us that God is FOR us, can empower us to hold on through tough times. God gave us our dreams because HE wants those dreams to come to pass, usually more than we do!

All that time that Joseph had spent in the pit and the prison, all the feelings of despair, it was all for this one moment. God had been orchestrating it all behind the scenes. Joseph's trust in God was truly being put to the test, and God proved Himself faithful time and time again.

This one verse vindicates all of Joseph's frustrations:

"So the advice was good in the eyes of Pharaoh and in the eyes of all of his servants. "Can we find such a one as this, a man in whom is the Spirit of God?"
Genesis 41:37–38

You may be feeling like you are still in the pit or the prison, but God is working tirelessly behind the scenes of your purpose. He may be hiding you for a season, but He WILL reveal you when you are ready and publicly prove the power of His Spirit in and through you. He is forming you, forging you to be a carrier of His Spirit.

Trusting God means trusting His timing.

Are You Ready for This?

God is into a little something I like to call, "the process." I have never enjoyed this "process" but over the years, I have realized that it is vital to my growth as a leader.

So often, we want our dream to come to pass NOW. I have heard it said, "We are a microwave generation serving a crock-pot God." This is so true, especially for leaders in this day and age. Because we have been given glimpses of our destinies, many times, we feel like everything should happen now. The reality is that God knows when we are ready to handle the fullness of our call and when we still need to be in process.

You may want to have immense influence, but think of those who are constantly in the spotlight. Forget the glam and the flash for a second and think about how much hate is directed toward those people on a daily basis. Whether it is through social media, email, tabloids, or gossip, people of great influence come under great scrutiny, even when they are trying to do good for the world and their community.

While you are busy asking for greater influence, the Lord is asking you, "Could you really handle that right now?" When you really think about it, could you handle the amount of criticism that those who are living in your desired calling are able to handle? What would you do when hundreds and thousands of people are pulling on your time and you have to ignore the majority of them? Are you *really* ready for it?

I have realized that every mistake, every moment of weakness and every pit-stop in my life is a vital part of my process and is creating in me the strength to one day carry out the dream I was given many years ago.

Do not get discouraged with where you are at, right now. It is all a part of the process, and you will never be able to go back to this place when are fully carrying the call that God promised you. He is not in a rush (although we often think that He is).

***God is not as concerned with depending on you
as He is developing you.***

What Promotion Really Looks Like

I believe there is a hidden secret in Joseph's journey found by looking at his story in its entirety. I would submit to you that, although promotion is a powerful thing, it is not always what it appears to be.

Remember when we talked about how favor looks different in different seasons? I think the same is true about promotion. Sometimes we receive a promise that seems to lead to a promotion, yet it can be the very thing that leads us to a pit or a prison. How? Well, look at Joseph's life. His father promoted him with a robe, but that robe only led him to the pit.

Potiphar promoted Joseph with influence and power, but that only led to the prison.

So where did the promotion come from? It certainly did not come from the robe, or from royalty. Those two things led only to Joseph's greatest trials. They seemed to be 'objects of promotion' but they actually led to some of the greatest *demotions* of his life.

You see promotion never came from a robe or from royalty. Those were just earthly incentives.

Promotion came from the pit and the prison.

This is why Joseph's "pit-stops" were absolute necessities to create opportunities for him to fulfill his purpose. Favor and promotion led Joseph to the worst moments of his life. It was in these places the only truths he could cling to were the promises of God. Both pit stops were simply detours, vehicles if you will, to launch Joseph into the place he was destined to be. Those pits were filled with pain, and yet it was in the midst of that pain that the Comforter revealed Himself, and turned the pain into purpose.

The "Joseph" who endured through the pit and the prison would no longer rely on his abilities, connections, or ambitions; he would now rely on the power of the Spirit upon him to lead him into his calling. Only through the process would this dependence on God truly take place, and it most certainly did.

God is sovereign over your process,
and it is in your process that God creates power.

There's the process again! It is hardly ever something we desire to be a part of. Have you ever had to take a long road trip, cooped up in a car for hours on end? Unfortunately, I have had the privilege of driving across the country in my small Honda Accord.

I drove my car from New York to Texas before my second year at Bible school had started. It was a grueling, twenty-five-hour drive. At the time, I was dating a girl who decided to come with me, along with her sister and her mother. Needless to say, I was outnumbered.

I have noticed something over the years. Men have a tendency to want to get somewhere right away. This means as little stops as possible. Women, on the other hand, like to stop and "see" things. Well, on this trip, I had no choice. What could have been a straight-shot trip took three and a half days. We stopped more than I thought possible. All I wanted was to get to Dallas as soon as possible and these girls were moving at the speed of snail!

A couple of years later, I drove my car from Redding, California, back to Texas. I planned to drive by myself so I was excited to straight-shoot it all the way there, however, I realized about seven hours in that I was not cut out for the long trip all at once. I ended up stopping three times and breaking up the trip into two days. Although I did not get to Texas as fast as I wanted to, I got to enjoy some beautiful sights along the way and reconnect with old friends.

God has shown me that our journey to purpose is a mixture between the two ideas of travel: we can make so many stops along the way that we delay ourselves from getting to where God wants us to go, but in our haste to get to the destination, we can rush past incredible opportunities to experience on the way. It is somewhere in the middle that God desires us to live in to fully embrace the process.

If you are wondering when you are going to get to where God has called you to go, know that He has not abandoned you or forgotten you. He did not give you those dreams in vain. He knows what you need to get you where you are going. Sometimes it is a pit and sometimes it is a palace, but whatever God chooses to use in your life, know that it is all a part of the grand design to bring you into the fullness of His goodness. God has great plans for you. Sometimes we cannot see the fullness of those plans, but trusting in the Lord strengthens us to carry out the call that He has given us. He is writing our miracle-story.

And it does not end there. To quote one of my spiritual mentors, Pastor Jaycee Jennings, "the best is yet to come."

Activation:

God is sovereign over your process. Even in the moments when you feel abandoned and forgotten, He is working all things together for your good. Where have you seen God pull you from your own pit and bring you into promise? Take some time to write down testimonies of God's faithfulness to your process and go back over them to remind your spirit of who your God is!

Prayer:

God, thank You for Your faithfulness. Thank You that You have never left me nor forsaken me. I choose to trust in Your goodness today. Even when I cannot see the big picture!

16

God's plan: ultimate restoration

Y ou may have thought that we arrived at "happily ever after," but there is still one more test that Joseph had to pass, and it is the ultimate test that was waiting for him on his front door.

Before I point out the last test, I believe there is a very powerful key that is hidden in this story. As you remember, Joseph's dreams are what got him into this mess in the first place. He was a dreamer who desired earnestly to see those dreams become a reality.

Have you ever noticed that the dreamer (Joseph) is called upon consistently to interpret and to serve other people's dreams throughout this story? Joseph interprets the dreams of the baker, the butler AND Pharaoh. The guy who started with a dream is now being used to interpret the dreams of others and all the while, he has yet to see his own come to life!

If we desire to see our own dreams come to life, we must first learn to celebrate and serve the dreams of others.

Even though Joseph had his OWN dream from God, he had to prove that he could first be faithful with the dreams of those around him. It was not enough to just interpret these dreams, God called him a step further to actually *serve* Pharaoh's dream. This meant years of putting his *own* dream on the back burner to use all of his efforts to serve someone else.

I have heard it said, "To have authority one must be under authority." I would say the same is true about dreams. If God has called you to a great purpose, He will often times place you in a position to serve someone else's dream. This is far from punishment; it is God's way of testing your ability to steward and celebrate someone else's dream. Only until you are able to serve someone else's dream can God trust you with your own.

And so he does. After Joseph interprets Pharaoh's dream by revealing that there would be a great famine coming to the land, he gave instructions on how to prepare for it by storing up one fifth of the land's produce and rationing out portions to the people during the years of lack. He serves Pharaoh's dream and gets so caught up in it that he forgets that the God of *HIS* dream is already working behind the scenes.

Sure enough, immediately following the seven years of plenty, a great famine struck the land and all of the surrounding regions, including the region where Joseph's family lived.

When Jacob (Joseph's father) heard that Egypt had been storing food for seven years in preparation for the famine, he commanded Joseph's brothers to journey there in hopes of receiving rations for their family. They had no idea that they would actually come face-to-face with their brother.

Completely unaware that he was in power, or even alive for that matter, they set out for Egypt. They entered the city and approached the man in charge of the entire Egyptian society, their brother. They bowed before him, completely unaware that their bloodline stood right in front of them.

Backtrack with me for a second, this was Joseph's original dream. Do you remember the sheaves of wheat and clusters of stars bowing down to him? Joseph's purpose is unfolding right before his eyes. It is all beginning to make sense, but at what cost?

The Dread of the Dream

Just imagine this for a second: the brothers who were supposed to love and protect you did everything in their power to eliminate you. They sold you into slavery and told your father that you were dead. Now, years later, they are standing on your doorstep, completely unaware that they are speaking to you, and are asking for food so that they can survive the famine. They are begging for your mercy to stay alive. Oh, the irony.

In a moment, a swarm of emotions flooded his heart. He recognized his brothers and spun around to hide his face.

Can this be? Is it really them? Is this my chance to finally get revenge for all of the hell they put me through?

He held back the tears as a lump in his throat began to swell up.

Instead of giving them what they wanted or ignoring them completely, Joseph decides to mess with them a little bit. He treats them as strangers and calls them spies (to read along, see Exodus 41). After watching them cower in fear, he decides to answer their cry and send them with grain in their sacks. He does not even take their money; however, he demands a payment that could not be bought with silver or gold. He commands them to bring back their youngest brother, Benjamin and until they followed through on this request, Joseph would keep his brother, Simeon in jail. An eye for an eye, right?

Joseph waited patiently until his brothers finally returned with their youngest brother, Benjamin. This time they made sure they brought all they needed to get out of Egypt with everyone intact, so they offered double the money, just in case they needed to pay off their debts. But, Joseph was not going to let them off that easy. He invites them to dine with him that night and sets their minds and stomachs at ease. They filled their mouths with food, with Benjamin, enjoying a portion five times the size of the others' (signifying favor). Joseph's appetite, however, is nonexistent. He is sitting across the table from the very men who desired to kill him. He asks himself if he is truly ready to let go and forgive their debt.

Being wise among men, Joseph comes up with a plan to see if his brothers have had a true change of heart. He orders his servants to fill their sacks with grain and to return their money for a second time but, he gives one servant a special instruction to hide the royal, silver cup in Benjamin's sack.

Just as his brothers are about to leave, he orders his men to search their sacks for stolen possessions. Sure enough, Joseph's guards find the royal, silver cup in Benjamin's bag. Joseph orders that Benjamin be punished, but just as he is about to take him into custody, something extraordinary happens. Judah, one of Joseph's brothers, cries out for mercy.

"Please, do not hurt the boy! My father has had two sons during his old age. The first was lost and now, if Benjamin does not return with us, my father will surely disown me. He has given this boy into our hands, trusting us to protect him. Please, have mercy!"

Joseph's worst nightmare has come true. The very same man who threw him into the pit and betrayed him into slavery is now defending his little brother. It was all a part of Joseph's test, but he had never expected them to pass! What had changed? What was wrong with Joseph that his brothers would defend Benjamin but not him?

He commands everyone to leave the room and with the last slam of his chamber's door, he falls to the ground and weeps bitterly. All of the rejection is rushing back in and spitting in his face.

"So this is how you repay me, God? They would save this young boy but not me? Why are you showing me this? Why did I have to be the scapegoat?

To be people of purpose, we must expect nothing in return, except what God desires to give to us.

In these times we realize that the people God has called us to serve are the same ones who will honor anyone other than us! We may have sacrificed more than they could ever imagine yet our voice seems to be the only one left unheard.

The Sower

Have you ever experienced this? As a pastor, I have many times felt as if my congregation will listen to anyone other than me. I can say something for months, and someone else unknown to them says the very same thing and they receive it passionately as if they are hearing it for the first time.

Being a forerunner sometimes means being the sower of the seed, while someone else is the reaper. Joseph set his brothers up to see if they would do the very same thing to Benjamin that they did to him. He made them give up one of their own to go and retrieve him, and once he was in Joseph's presence, he was favored more than all of his brothers. His dinner portion was FIVE TIMES the size of everyone else's, which was quite a blessing in a time of famine.

No doubt, the brothers noticed Benjamin's plate, yet this time, his favor did not threaten them. Instead of willingly offering him up due to their jealousy, they surrounded him in brotherly love and protection, demanding that his life be spared.

As Joseph wept himself into the carpet, he was reminded of the tears he had shed at the bottom of the pit. All of his anger and hurt came bubbling up to the surface, and all he could do was cry. Why did he have to be the scapegoat? Why did he have to be the one that was thrown into the pit? Why could they not have learned this lesson before they betrayed him?

In the midst of the tears and the cries, Joseph remembered the voice he heard at the bottom of the pit. It was that same voice that was speaking so softly to him now:

"Joseph, this *is* the dream that I gave you. You were made for such a time as this. It is because of *you* that your brothers have been reborn and their hearts of stone have become hearts of flesh. It is because of *your* life that they now can enter into restoration, and I smile upon them because I smile upon you. They are in an emotional pit right now. Will you rescue them even though they did not rescue you?"

You see Joseph was the one who ended up teaching his brothers to protect and cherish their own. They had seen the pain that their father experienced with the loss of his son Joseph, and they never wanted to put him through that again. They knew now that even though the youngest had more favor, they were to guard and defend that favor instead of competing with it.

Yet Joseph could not help but feel gypped out of his own investment. They were sorrowful *now* and would do anything to protect *Benjamin,* but why could not they have done that for him? Why did he have to be the one that God used to teach them this lesson?

As young leaders, we answer the call to our purpose by pioneering new territories. To lead the way, one must break up hard ground and push through things that others will never understand, or perhaps even see. The leader may never get to eat the fruit of his or her labor. That is the sacrifice of a forerunner.

Full Circle

It was in this moment that Joseph had a decision to make: would he seek revenge and smite them for their blatant disregard for his life or would he fulfill his purpose and bring salvation and restoration to his family?

After getting up and wiping the tears from his eyes, Joseph calls his brothers back, and reveals his identity to them. They fall to the floor in shock, terror and disbelief, all at the same time. Could this be? Could this be the brother they betrayed? Would they return to their father with not one but *two* of his favored sons, or would he kill them on the spot?

They begged and pleaded for mercy, but Joseph had made up his mind. He had passed his test. He was not going to harm them; he was not going to seek revenge. From past experience, Joseph knew that living out his calling was always more worthwhile than taking things into his own hands.

You see Joseph had been here before. Just like the spiritual, spiral staircase, he had faced this test only a few steps prior to his current situation. Where, you might ask? I am so glad you did.

It was shortly after Joseph was released from prison and put into the highest place of power under the Pharaoh. He was setting up his royal quarters when the butler walked in to apologize for his lapse of memory.

It was at that moment that Joseph had to face the test of forgiveness. Now, with the power to wipe this guy off the face of the earth, he had a decision to make: restoration or revenge?

He may have faced this test unwillingly, but he had already faced the pain of rejection and abandonment, and chose to forgive. All of that was preparation for this one moment: the redemption of broken brotherhood and forgotten family.

Not only does Joseph reveal his identity to his brothers, he reveals his heart and the power of the Spirit of God at work in him as he embraces the ones who once threw him into a pit. Instead of banishing them, Joseph brings his entire family to Egypt, including his father, and restores what was lost in his family.

All of Joseph's training was for this one purpose, this final test. He had passed the test of the pit and the prison. He had passed the test of success and seduction. He was given favor beyond measure, but it all meant nothing if he could not forgive and love the ones who hurt him the most. He was ready. He began to open his mouth . . .

And then . . . he remembered the dreams he saw all those years ago. He saw the stars and the stalks, and what he thought they meant all of a sudden to mean a completely different thing.

It was as if the pieces of the puzzle of his purpose were all coming into alignment for the first time. He could see it clearly now. Before, he had to much anger—too much pride. He would have abused his power and forced his brothers to fall on their knees before him. But now, staring at them through tears that burned in his eyes, he realized what brokenness had done in his heart all these years later.

It all made sense now. His call to go higher was a call to go lower.

His journey would have been meaningless if he could not look his betrayers in the eyes and forgive them. It was the original dream that God gave him, yet he never would have expected it to happen this way.

It is rarely as easy as we think it will be, yet, the way God goes about teaching us how to love is one of the most powerful and softening processes we could ever experience. It is the highest honor to attend the school of humility and brokenness.

Joseph attended this school, and as a result was able to say this at the end of the story:

*Joseph said to them, "Do not be afraid, for am I in the place of God? **But as for you, you meant evil against me; but God meant it for good, in order to bring it about as it is this day, to save many people alive.***
Genesis 50:19–20

God's purpose for his life was never about his brothers bowing down to him. It was never about him being in charge or being a big shot.

God's purpose for Joseph was to rise to a higher level so that he could one day serve his brothers once more.

It all made sense now. His call to leadership was a call to be a servant.

God's plan: ultimate restoration.

17

the perspective of purpose: yes.

I hope that by now, you can realize the power of Joseph's yes in each and every season. Your "yes" will lead you to God's purpose for your life, and I can promise you—it is greater than you can ever imagine.

God's ultimate plan is not to simply elevate you to a place of influence and power to accomplish in the earth the things He desires. God can do all of those things perfectly well by Himself. No, God's ultimate desire for you is not ministry, leadership or government.

God's ultimate desire for you is that you would learn to love and serve others because Christ loved and served you.

All this is from God who reconciled us to Himself through Christ Jesus and also gave us the ministry of reconciliation.
2 Corinthians 5:18

Favor is never to exalt self; in fact, it is simply the opposite. Favor is so undeserved that I believe it is God's greatest form of discipline in our lives. We alone can see our undeserving hearts yet through God's grace, He lavishes His love and blessing upon us. We might wonder what we did to get God to love us so much.

Here's the kicker: *we had nothing to do with it, and that is what glorifies Him the most.*

God's desire is to love so unconditionally and so radically that it melts the hardest heart into a form that He can use to love others.

We are God's answer to hard hearts, but the answer is not found in power or authority, it is found in humility and brokenness that come from the process, from the pit to the palace.

God's purpose for your life will take you further than you imagined and will exceed every expectation that you could ever dream of, yet it is rarely ever the road we thought we would walk. It was through many trials that Joseph's purpose was formed, but the promise that awaited him was so incredibly worthwhile.

Life with God is the most remarkable adventure you can embark upon. Through His Spirit in you, God can redeem all that has been lost and all that has been broken from a life willing to trust God, even in valley of the shadow of death. The call is truly beyond what you could ever ask or think.

So the question is, will you answer the call even when the road is nothing like you expected? Will you say yes to the divine invitation to a radical connection with the heart of God? Will you choose to lay down your life for others, even those who have betrayed you? Will you partner with God in seeing the redemption of a lost world and offer Jesus the full reward of His sufferings?

Young leader, this is your purpose: to be a miracle, made only possible through a life lived for God. The road may be narrow and only a few may find it, but the road of the righteous leads to unprecedented promises.

It's a simple response, but yields radical results.

Just. Say. Yes.

about the author

J ared Ellis was called into ministry at the age of sixteen, after being delivered out of a life of darkness, depression, and depravity. He has traveled all over the world, preaching the good news of Jesus Christ and has worked with some of the leading churches in the nation, such as Bethel Church and Elevation Church. He pastored in Abilene, Texas for three years and grew a youth ministry of twelve students to over 300—signs, wonders, and miracles happening each week. He currently travels full-time as an evangelist and preaches at churches, conferences, and events. He is also the GE Director at Christ for The Nations Institute where he teaches and trains Youth Pastors. While at home in Dallas, Texas, he serves as a worship leader at Trinity Church.

For booking and contact information, visit www.jaredellis.us/booking.

CPSIA information can be obtained
at www.ICGtesting.com
Printed in the USA
FFOW01n1835110716
25761FF